FREE SOFTWARE FOR YOUR TI HOME COMPUTER

David Heller
Dorothy Heller

ENRICH/OHAUS
San Jose, California

Graphic Design by Kaye Graphics
Illustrations by Corb Hillam

Edited by Matt Foley
Assistant Editors Eldon Kerr, John Deubert and Erich Winkler

Typography by KGN Graphics

Published by
ENRICH/OHAUS
2325 Paragon Drive
San Jose, CA 95131
U.S.A.

For information on rights and distribution outside the U.S.A., please write ENRICH/OHAUS at the above address.

ISBN: 0-86582-124-0
Catalog No. EN79214
Printed in the United States of America
10 9 8 7 6 5 4 3 2

Disclaimer of Warranties and Limitation of Liabilities

The authors have taken due care in preparing this book and the programs in it, including research, development, and testing to ascertain their effectiveness. The authors and the publisher make no expressed or implied warranty of any kind with regard to these programs or the supplementary documentation of this book. In no event shall the authors or the publishers be liable for incidental or consequential damages in connection with or arising out of the furnishing, performance, or use of any of these programs and other materials in this book.

ABOUT THE AUTHORS

Dorothy and David Heller believe that computers can be understandable and accessible to everyone! They specialize in books that help people get more enjoyment and utility from their computers. David is co-author of *Dr. Wacko's Miracle Guide to Designing and Programming Your Own Atari Computer Arcade Games* (Addison-Wesley, 1983); *Space Knights* a science fiction novel with nine interactive games for the Atari computer (Reston, 1983); and is a frequent contributor to *Hi-Res, Atari Connection,* and *InfoWorld.*

Dorothy is co-author of *Computer Confidence: A Guide for Women* (Acropolis, 1983); *PET Games and Recreation* (Reston, 1981); and is a frequent contributor to *Hi-Res, Atari Connection, InfoWorld, Compute,* and *Interface Age.*

ACKNOWLEDGEMENTS

The generous and enthusiastic help from many Users' Group officers, educators, and the people at TI Computers, has made this book a reality. Thank you very much for your support and words of wisdom.

We'd like to say a special "thank you" to Mr. Ralph Fowler, operator of the T.I.B.B.S for his telecommunications technical help and advice.

Many thanks to Mr. Ed Wiest of TI for all his help.

TABLE OF CONTENTS

INTRODUCTION

ENRICH YOUR TI COMPUTING EXPERIENCE
WITH
FREE SOFTWARE FOR YOUR TI

- Shows you where to find valuable free resources for you and your TI computer.

Users' Groups

- Introduces you to the exciting world of TI Users' Groups. There are more than 160 of these groups WORLDWIDE offering extensive Free Software libraries, courses, informative newsletters, terrific discounts on TI-related equipment and software, and help for everyone from complete beginners to sophisticated programmers.

Free Software by Phone

- Shows you how to get FREE programs, by phone, without leaving your home!

- Introduces you to the exciting world of telecommunications and explains all the terms and concepts you need.

- Directory lists over 500 phone numbers that enable you to telecommunicate with other computer users all over the world.

- Introduces you to the first exclusively TI Bulletin Board Service, an exciting new development for TI owners everywhere!

Start your own Bulletin Board Service

- The creator of the first "electronic Bulletin Board" exclusively for TI 99ers tells you how to start your own "base" station, and how to get the software you'll need.

Attention—Parents and Educators

- Shows you where to find the support you'll need to expand the use of your TI computer at home and in the classroom. We also show you how and where to get FREE educational software, and how to network with other parents and teachers to solve teaching problems, and to share ideas and programs.

- A special section on TI LOGO explains the features and benefits of this "language for learning"—and introduces you to free resources for educational support and software!

Looking for the right magazine?

- Gives you a directory of magazines for TI computer owners, with subscription information.

*** *AND MUCH, MUCH MORE* ***

A WORD AGAINST PIRACY

This book has been written to show you how to obtain free software *without* resorting to piracy.

Piracy is the theft of copyrighted software by unauthorized copying and distribution.

Piracy is not only illegal and immoral. . .it can actually drive a small software house out of business, destroy individual creative incentive, and make larger companies unwilling to make the investment required to produce high quality software.

Piracy can deprive you of a large software selection at the marketplace, and make it hard for you to pursue a job career as a professional programmer.

The overall result of piracy is to punish those who produce excellent software and encourage those who produce quick and dirty software.

When you buy programs from a reliable software house, you'll get the support you need to get the most out of their product. Customer service, documentation, updates, revision notices all cost money. The pirate can't offer any of these services. A thief can only sell you what has been stolen. . .then you're on your own.

WELCOME
TO FREE
SOFTWARE
FOR YOUR TI COMPUTER

WELCOME TO FREE SOFTWARE AND RESOURCES FOR YOUR TI COMPUTER

TI 99/4 & 99/4A™ OWNERS

NO MATTER WHERE YOU LIVE

No matter where you live—in the U.S. of A., Canada, England, Europe, Australia, or even the Azores—we'll show you how to get FREE software and access many valuable resources for you and your TI computer.

USERS' GROUPS: ONE GREAT RESOURCE

The first section of *Free Software* introduces you to the exciting world of TI Users' Groups. There are more than 160 of these groups WORLDWIDE offering extensive Free Software libraries, courses, informative newsletters, and help for TI owners. Many of these groups have special interests. Our detailed profiles of selected groups introduce you to clubs that offer educational software, support for the handicapped, hotline assistance for programmers, computer literacy tutorials, terrific discounts on TI-related equipment and software—and much, much more!

We've listed ALL the clubs, WORLDWIDE, and tell you how to become a member of many of these groups without leaving your home! Or, if you'd like, we show you where your nearest group is, and the right person to contact, so you can attend their next meeting and get FREE software and support from other TI owners.

START YOUR OWN TI USERS' GROUP!

We even show you how to start your own TI Users' Group, based on information from Texas Instruments' Ed Wiest, and advice from other 99ers who participate in Users' Groups in their areas.

SOFTWARE BY PHONE

Exciting new developments are taking place in the world of TI. The first electronic bulletin board services for TI users are going on-line as we write these words! FREE SOFTWARE BY PHONE explains the terms used in computer telecommunications, gives you a comprehensive equipment buyer's guide, and tells you how to turn your computer into a telecommunications terminal today!

We show you how to get FREE software by phone, send your programs to others or chat with distant computer owners.

We also tell you how to use your TI communications software to get on-line with the Source and TEXNET. For users who can take advantage of all the services the Source offers, TEXNET is an excellent value. Once you become a TEXNET member, you can download software for FREE from the TEXNET program library!

WHAT IF I DON'T OWN A MODEM?

What if you don't have a modem or peripheral expansion box? Don't worry! You can still enjoy lots of free resources for your TI 99/4A until you're ready to expand. Of course, you don't need a modem to simply order by phone or by mail from the extensive collections of TI 99/4A public domain software available from many Users' Groups and other resources.

When you are ready to expand your system, FREE SOFTWARE gives you all the information you need to select a good modem, get on-line, and take full advantage of the world of computer telecommunications.

SET UP YOUR OWN BASE STATION

In an exciting interview, the creator of the first exclusively TI "electronic Bulletin Board" tells you how to start your own "base" station, and how to get the software you'll need at a moderate cost!

FREE SOFTWARE introduces you to Atlanta's "T.I.B.B.S."—TI Bulletin Board Service—soon to be joined by other BBS's for TI 99/4A users.

OVER 500 FREE EXCHANGES TO CALL

As a bonus we've included an additional 500 phone numbers for you to explore! Although you can't exchange software by modem with non-TI computers, you CAN communicate with valuable resources. Once you get on-line, you can exchange technical information and a wealth of specialized knowledge with other computer users anywhere in the world.

ATTENTION—PARENTS & EDUCATORS FREE EDUCATIONAL SOFTWARE

Free Software is particularly valuable to parents and educators who use the TI computer in a learning environment. Our comprehensive section on Educational Software and Resources shows you where to find the support you need to expand the use of your TI computer at home and in the classroom. We also show you how and where to get FREE educational software, and how to network with other parents and teachers to solve teaching problems and share ideas and programs.

We discuss TI LOGO, the "language for learning"; the enhanced features of LOGO II; and the new resources and services that are springing up to support this exciting teaching tool—including FREE public domain educational software.

ALMOST FREE SOFTWARE

A directory of magazines for TI home computer owners, with subscription information and a synopsis of the type of material and FREE TI 99/4A software listings each magazine provides, is in our Almost Free Software section. Knowing which publications are best for your needs saves you time and expense while increasing the enjoyment and utility you'll get from your TI computer.

ENRICH YOUR COMPUTING EXPERIENCE

Regardless of your age, interests, or where you live, the valuable information in *Free Software* will expand and enrich your TI computing experience!

WHAT IS FREE SOFTWARE?

As TI Users' Groups have grown, many members have become increasingly familiar and proficient with their computers. An outgrowth of this experience is an abundance of user-written public domain programs for your TI computer.

Public domain software is a user's gift to you. It is software that has been donated to the public by its creator.

WHERE IS IT? HOW CAN I GET IT?

These valuable programs are in the libraries of TI Users' Groups throughout the world and are available to members and non-members alike for the cost of the disk or cassette, reproduction, and handling. No profit is built into this cost; the charge for a typical cassette loaded with as many as fifteen programs is usually between one to five dollars.

Even the groups that sell TI 99/4A-related equipment and commercial software for profit offer you selections from their public domain programs—for FREE!

You can get public domain software by mail, by visiting a neighborhood club, or by using a modem to "ask" an electronic Bulletin Board to send the program to you over the phone lines. The first user-owned and operated TI 99/4A bulletin board service that will enable you to download and exchange public domain software is going on-line as we write this book!

TEXNET members can also exchange software by modem to take advantage of the public domain programs this service offers. (Our "Free Software By Phone" section shows you how to do this.)

WHAT IS IT WORTH?

What's free public domain software worth? The answer is. . . a lot! Public domain software allows you to build a useful and diverse software library without spending a fortune or resorting to piracy.

Most public domain software can't replace the skills and expertise that professionals bring to heavy business application software. There are times when you'll be happy to spend what a commercial software company asks. . . their product will justify your investment.

Programs like TI Writer™, Multiplan™, and Securities Analysis™, are examples of professional work that would be difficult to find in the public domain arena.

But what about all those other applications? Some of the best game, educational, and home management software is available free, and if you're a computer programmer the choice of excellent public domain programming aids and utility software is almost endless.

Then there are those times when your kids want ten new games a month, or you need more software for your classroom than your school district can afford, or you want to take a look at a program's listing to learn more about programming. Public domain software to the rescue!

Public domain software:

- is useful, and enjoyable. . . there are free programs that range from games to home management to education.

- is really valuable. Although most public domain programs are not quite as polished as their commercial counterparts, many are just perfect for *your* special application. And, they're free!

- enables you to take advantage of the special applications knowledge and experience of different users—like programs that another parent has developed for a special learning disabled kid, or a program for home management that another TI home computer owner developed that's perfect for your needs.

- teaches you how to judge commercial software. After you've been exposed to a variety of public domain programs, you'll know the difference between a good commercial product and one that really isn't worth your money. When you do decide to invest in a commercial product, you'll be an educated buyer; you'll get the best value.

NO MATTER WHERE YOU LIVE

No matter where you live, you'll be able to get free software by mail by simply writing to many of the clubs listed in our TI Users' Club Directory.

Ask for their catalog of public domain software. If they have one, they'll be happy to send it to you.

TI Users' Groups offer a surprising variety of valuable information and software. The well-known International 99/4 Users' Group has more than 400 educational programs, and the 99/4A Users of America offer special software for visually-impaired computer users that can open up a whole new world for physically handicapped 99ers!

Many other clubs that aren't as well known also offer lots of software goodies. One club, the 99/4 Computer Users' Group in Atlanta, Georgia, offers more than 700 programs in a variety of categories!

Atlanta's Program Exchange Library is typical of the software services that many TI Users' Groups are offering. The Exchange Library is designed to allow the sharing of user-written programs. There are two ways to get programs from the Atlanta 99/4A Computer Users' Program Exchange:

(1) Order the cassette(s) or disk(s) and enclose the appropriate amount of money (only $2-4 per program).

(2) Send the Atlanta group a program(s) you've written and want to share with other enthusiasts. In exchange, the group will send you any three programs of your choice. *The Atlanta 99/4A Users' Group strongly supports this second way of adding programs to their library, and will go out of their way to help you share your programs with others.*

The Atlanta 99/4A Computer Users' Group is representative of the many clubs that will send public domain software to you by mail.

WHAT TYPE OF SOFTWARE IS AVAILABLE?

A wide variety of FREE software is now currently available. No matter where your interests lie, there's something for you!

GAMES
BUSINESS
EDUCATION
HOME MANAGEMENT
COMPUTER UTILITIES
GRAPHICS DEMONSTRATIONS
SOUND AND MUSIC PROGRAMS

The following list, from the Atlanta 99/4A Users' Group Exchange Library is representative of the many choices available to you. New programs are being added daily, and this list only shows a fraction of the public domain software available.

ATLANTA 99/4A USERS' GROUP

PROGRAM LIBRARY

All of the programs listed in this catalog have been submitted as part of our software exchange policy or reproduced from public domain. The Users' Group does not claim proprietary rights to any of these programs and cannot be held responsible for their content. Anyone finding an error in any of these programs should provide us with the corrections so that we may make them available to all members.

• BUSINESS/PROFESSIONAL •

BS0001 ADDRESSES1 (DISK, PRINT)
File hundreds of names and addresses on a single disk. Alphabetizes names.

BS0002 ADDRESSES2 (XB, DISK, PRINT)
Extended basic version of above program.

BS0003 COLUMNAR PAD (XB, PRINT)
Extended basic. Simulates a columnar pad with descriptive column and seven numerical columns.

BS0004 DEPRECIATE1
Calculates straight line depreciation. You specify variables.

BS0005 DEPRECIATE2 (XB)
Extended basic version of above program.

BS0006 FINANCIAL MATH
Interests and annuities. Good program.

BS0007 INVESTMENT CALCULATOR
Excellent program to calculate different financial sets.

BS0008 MAIL LIST1
Add, delete, search, and update names using cassette tape.

BS0009 MAIL LIST2 (XB, DISK)
Extended basic disk version of above program.

BS0010 WORD PROCESSING (PRINTER SUGGESTED)
Allows upper and lower case with editing.

BS0011 TEX SCRIBE (XB, PRINT)
Turn your 99/4A into a word processor. Can utilize extra memory if available.

DM0001 BASIC DEMO
Demo of sound and graphics depicting TI's 1979 annual report.

DM0002 BOUNCE BALL
Bouncing ball demo. Can be enhanced into a pong game.

DM0003 CALENDAR
Displays calendar of any month on your screen.

DM0004 CHARDEF1
Helps define 8x8 block graphic characters.

DM0005 CHARDEF2 (XB)
Extended basic version of above program.

DM0006 COLOR CRAYON (DISK)
Draw your own creations on the screen and save it on disk.

DM0007 COLOR CRAYON (TAPE)
Same as above using cassette tape.

DM0008 LOVE POSTER (PRINT Opt.)
Displays a poster of Robert Indiana's famous 'LOVE' design.

DM0009 MARQUEE
Displays colorful vertical bars on the screen while generating random tones.

DM0010 ROBOT JOKES (TEII, SPEECH)
Rocky Robot tells hilarious robot jokes.

DM0011 SNOOPY XMAS
A graphic rendition of the famous beagle by his Christmas tree.

DM0012 SNOOPY XMAS2 (XB)
Snoopy and his Christmas tree. Plays 'The First Noel'.

DM0013 SPRITE DEMO (XB)
One of the best sprite demos available. Show off the 99/4A's capabilities.

DM0014 SPRITER DEMO (XB)
Demo of 'SPRITER' capabilities.

DM0015 JUMPING SPRITES (XB)
Demo of sprites jumping over each other.

• EDUCATIONAL PROGRAMS •

ED0001 STATES AND NATIONS
4 versions of a question/answer game. Works with states/capitals or nations/capitals.

ED0002 HOMEWORK HELPER—FRACTIONS
Several variations of working with fractions. Good graphics and sound.

ED0003 HOMEWORK HELPER—DIVISION
Several variations of working with division. Good graphics and sound.

ED0004 NAME THAT BONE
Computer displays skeleton with names of bones. Name them correctly from memory. Good graphics.

ED0005 MYSTERY WORDS
Learn to read music by guessing the mystery word displayed as musical notes on a staff.

ED0006 ROCKY ROBOT (SPEED & TEII REQUIRED)
Nursery rhymes are recited by Rocky.

ED0007 BIORHYTHMS
Display your biorhythm using color charts.

ED0008 CAPITOLS
A good guessing game to test your knowledge of the capitals of all 50 states.

ED0009 HAPPY SPELL (SPEECH & TEII REQUIRED)
Spelling drill by the computer using the words you have entered. Mistakes are repeated.

ED0010 MORSE CODE
Learn morse code the easy way with your 99/4A.

ED0011 PRESIDENTS II
Test your ability to name all the presidents in the order of their term in office.

ED0012 SPEAK & SPELL FLASH 2 (SPEECH & TEII REQUIRED)
Flashes a word on the screen then speaks it. You must then spell it from memory.

ED0013 SPEAK & SPELL FLASH 3 (SPEECH & TEII REQUIRED)
Next level of the above program.

ED0014 TYPING TUTOR
You input the letters you wish to practice and the computer tests you.

ED0015 TYPING FOR ACCURACY
Allows you to specify which typing fingers you want to exercise.

ED0016 WORLD FLAGS
A very good program that depicts the flags of 29 nations. Test of memory and recognition.

GM0001 BATTLE AT SEA
Command your fleet of warships in a duel with the computer's fleet.

GM0002 SPACE INVADERS
Variation of TI INVADERS with multiple warheads. Keyboard controls movement, firing.

GM0003 ENEMY ATTACK
Your jet must fight off attack of enemy squadron. Use arrow keys to move, ENTER key to fire.

GM0004 HARRIED HOUSEWIFE
Make gameboard matches from memory. Similar to TV game of 'CONCENTRATION'. Good graphics.

GM0005 MEMORY EXPANSION
Memory test. Computer displays random sequence of numbers/letters, you must repeat from memory.

GM0006 TEX THELLO
Game of strategy, 3 levels of difficulty. Try to capture the most squares on a grid. 1-2 players.

GM0007 MAZE RACE
2 player game. A race to guide your soldier thru the maze. Avoid your enemy or both will die.

GM0008 SAN FRANCISCO TOURIST
2 games: 1) Drive your car down the crookedest street in S.F. 2) Mark trees in Muir Woods.

GM0009 SLOT MACHINE
Try your luck on a casino slot machine without losing too many points.

GM0010 DRAGON MAZE
Negotiate invisible maze to reach the other side before the dragon gets you.

GM0011 ARTILLERY
Cannon duel with enemy. Your scouts have given you enemy position. You control cannon elevation.

GM0012 DODGE 'EM (XB)
Cross busy intersection while avoiding oncoming traffic. Elapsed time and crash count kept.

GM0013 INTERPLANETARY RESCUE (XB)
Pilot your landing vehicle to a safe landing. Choose level of difficulty and planets.

GM0014 CODE BREAKER (XB)
Guess the secret code. Computer tells you the # of correct characters and # in right position.

GM0015 FORCE I (XB)
Maneuver your ship and set gun sights on alien ship and fire. Good graphics.

GM0016 SPACE PATROL (XB, JSKT Opt.)
Destroy enemy supply ships before they reach their battle-star. Avoid killer satellites.

GM0017 N-VADER (XB, JSTK Opt.)
1 or 2 players prevent alien creatures from reaching earth. You set game options.

GM0018 BATTLE STAR (XB)
Defend your battle star from 4 sided enemy attack. Use arrow keys to fire lasers.

GM0019 GOLF (XB, JSKT Opt.)
1 or 2 player game of golf. Avoid trees and water hazards to get to green.

GM0020 DRYWELL (XB)
Try to strike it rich by sinking oil wells in 36 acres of land. Guess where and how deep.

GM0021 SPACE GEM (XB)
Try your best to avoid enemy space ships. You set speed and skill level.

GM0022 STAR DODGER (XB)
Your ship and the computer's ship try to avoid asteroids. First to suffer a hit loses game.

GM0023 ZANQUEST (XB)
Your ship must reach the refueling station and destroy enemy fortress. Avoid patrols.

GM0024 GOLD RUSH (XB)
Dig through a mine in search of gold. You select skill level. Good graphics.

GM0025 A DAY AT THE RACES (XB)
Choose your favorite horse. Odds are given. Computer runs race and provides results.

GM0026 AIR TRAFFIC CONTROLLER (XB)
You are in command of a busy international airport. You control flights.

GM0027 AIR COMBAT (JSTCK)
Fly your plane off the deck of an aircraft carrier to do battle with enemy planes.

GM0028 ALIENS (JSTCK)
Shoot at the alien craft as they come across and down your screen.

GM0029 BATTLE FOR IAPETUS (JSTCK REQ)
An interesting graphic game in which you try to destroy your opponent's gun positions.

GM0030 BATTLESHIP
One player game. Sink all the enemy ships with the least amount of shots.

GM0031 BOXING (JSTCK)
Try to knock out your opponent in this terrific game.

GM0032 CAMEL
Try to cross the desert without killing the camel or yourself.

GM0033 CAR BASH
Drive a car around the screen while trying to run over the monsters.

GM0034 CARS & CARCASSES
Graphics/sound. Chase the monsters around the screen.

GM0035 CHECKERS
Play a graphic game of checkers against the 99/4A. Well written program.

GM0036 CHICKEN HELPER (XB)
Help the chicken get to the other side of the road.

GM0037 CIVIL WAR
Try to alter the course of history. You make strategic decisions.

GM0038 CONNECT FOUR
Similar to the Milton Bradley game. The object is to connect four.

GM0039 COUNTY FAIR DERBY
This program will show (graphically) a horse race.

GM0040 CRAPS
Graphics/sound. Place your bets and roll those bones.

GM0041 DEPTH CHARGE
Try to destroy the enemy ZORT submarine by dropping depth charges.

GM0042 DODGE 'EM 2
An excellent graphics maze game that you will enjoy.

GM0043 ENEMY ATTACK 2 (XB)
Waves of enemy planes are attacking. Will they advance or fire rockets?

GM0044 HOT-DOG (XB, JSTCK)
Hot Dog needs your help to cross the busy highway.

GM0045 INDIAN
A most challenging game of position and strategy. Ages 12 and over.

GM0046 INDY 500 (XB, JSTCK)
Pass on the inside or the outside, but you must avoid the other cars on the track.

GM0047 INVASION
This game was programmed in West Germany. An excellent game.

GM0048 MICRO JAWS (XB)
You are the great white shark, MICROJAWS. Swim up behind fish and gobble them up.

GM0049 MOLASSES MAN (XB)
All of the characters are there and so is the maze.

GM0050 MUGWUMP
Four mugwumps are hiding on a 10x10 grid. Try to find them.

GM0051 NIMBLE
Don't be the one caught with the last piece. Not as simple as it sounds.

GM0052 NOMAD
A 'TEXT' game. You must locate Grandma's house given clues by the computer.

GM0053 PARTY GAME
An adult board game of drinking, stripping, and fondling. Done in good taste.

GM0054 QUEST
The Granddaddy of all adventure games. Find your way out of a cave.

GM0055 RUSSIAN ROULETTE
Can you beat the odds in a game of Russian Roulette? Music and sound.

GM0056 SMILEY
Move around the screen gathering points while being chased by a smiley face.

GM0057 SPACE SCOUT
A great graphics space game. Your scout ship must pick up cargo pods.

GM0058 SPACE SCOUT 2 (XB, SPEECH)
The same great game as above in X-BASIC with speech.

GM0059 STAR FIGHT (JSTCK)
A difficult game to master, but one of the best space games yet.

GM0060 STAR TREK
A 'TEXT' game of Star Trek.

GM0061 STOCK MARKET
Play the stock market with the computer's money. Good simulation.

GM0062 SUPERMAN
A 'TEXT' game where you must destroy ten super villains hiding around the city.

GM0063 TAROT CARDS
The computer will deal the TAROT cards for you.

GM0064 TERMITE
Make the termite eat through a log, but watch out for knots.

GM0065 TI WARS
Graphics and music. A new and exciting space game.

GM0066 TICTACPEN (LIGHT PEN)
TIC-TAC-TOE against the computer using an easy to build light pen.

GM0067 TREK
Excellent graphics and sound. Shoot with phasers & torpedos. Impulse and warp drive.

GM0068 UP SCOPE (XB)
Torpedo the enemy ships before they drop depth charges on you.

GM0069 WAGON WHEEL
Save the girl in the burning wagon in Donkey Kong fashion.

GM0070 WALK IN THE WOODS
A super game that is fun for all ages. Walk in the woods and collect treasure.

GM0071 WHITE HOLES (JSTCK Opt.)
One of the best maze games yet. Find all the white holes and destroy them.

GM0072 YAHTZEE
Graphics and sound. This version of Milton Bradley's game of Yahtzee is fantastic.

GM0073 YAHTZEE JOY (JSTCK)
Same as the above game but using joysticks.

• HOME MANAGEMENT •

HM0001 CHECKBOOK
A simple checkbook system that lets you save the data on cassette tape.

HM0002 CHORES (PRINT)
Prints a chore list for your children (or spouse).

HM0003 HOME CHECK PROCESSOR (2 CASSETTE RECORDERS)
Allows you to file, sort, add and manipulate your checking account data.

HM0004 HOME SECRETARY/DIALER
Keeps phone list and household inventory.

HM0005 LISTS
Stores data for birthdays, appointments, etc. Uses data statements or cassette input.

HM0006 RECORD COLLECTION (XB, DISK, PRINT)
Allows you to store information about your record collection.

• MUSIC •

MU0001 YESTERDAY
BEATLE hit with words displayed. Good graphics.

MU0002 MAXWELL'S SILVER HAMMER
BEATLE tune.

MU0003 LUCY IN THE SKY WITH DIAMONDS
BEATLE tune.

MU0004 BEETHOVEN'S 9th
The haunting melody of this famous classic.

MU0005 BEWITCHED
Bewitched, Bothered, and Bewildered. An enchanting musical standard by Rodgers & Hart.

MU0006 BIRTHDAY
Plays the song in one part harmony.

MU0007 DOG GONE BOOGIE WOOGIE (XB)
A boogie woogie version of 'Where has my little dog gone'.

MU0008 GODFATHER
Music and graphics from the movie.

MU0009 INVENTION IN F
Make interesting variations to Bach's music by changing the volume and duration.

MU0010 M*A*S*H
Theme song with graphics.

MU0011 MUSIC BOX DANCER
Turn your 99/4A into a wonderful music box.

MU0012 MUSIC MAKER
Produce your own music and watch it projected on a musical scale.

MU0013 MUSIC EDIT
A music text editor. Requires MUSIC PLAY program to play back songs.

MU0014 MUSIC PLAY
Plays tunes created by MUSIC EDIT.

MU0015 MUSICTRANS
Music transposition table prints on screen.

MU0016 NEVER ON SUNDAY
Fantastic programming job. A tune the whole family will enjoy.

MU0017 PINK PANTHER
Theme song with graphics.

MU0018 STAR TREK
A well written version of the theme song.

• SCIENCE/ENGINEERING •

SC0001 AIRCRAFT PERFORMANCE (XB)
Calculates many factors used in the design of aircraft, including Ta, Tr, Pa, Pr.

SC0002 WEATHER STATION
Draws a station model based on information you provide. Not a program for amateurs.

• MISCELLANEOUS •

MS0001 AUTO-RUN (XB, DISK, MEMORY XPANSION)
Will automatically catalog raw disks and offers an auto run feature.

MS0002 DATABASE (DISK)
Allows easy storage and retrieval of data using disks.

MS0003 MAIL PREP (XB, DISK, TEII)
Used to create a letter file that can easily be dumped into SOURCE mail format.

MS0004 RECORDS (DISK)
Offers many search features and can be used as an accounts receivable program.

MS0005 SHRINK (XB, DISK)
Reduces the size of programs by removing REMS, shortening variable names, etc.

MS0006 SORTS
Contains a numeric shell sort and an alphabetic sort routine.

MS0007 SPEECH EDITOR (TEII)
Break words into allophones and construct new words.

MS0008 TE2CODE (XB, DISK, SPEECH)
Read back data that is stored on disk by the TEII module.

MS0009 VERBOSE (XB, DISK, SPEECH)
Make new words by combining words from XB.

MS0010 AUTOLOGON (TEII, DISK)
Generates an automatic log on file for use with the TEII module and TEXNET.

ATLANTA 99/4A USERS' GROUP LIBRARY EXCHANGE AGREEMENT

PROGRAM LIBRARY

You may obtain programs from the library by one of two methods:

1. *PURCHASE:* Any program in this catalog may be selected for a nominal service charge to cover our cost of operation. Members pay $3 for the first program per order, every additional program will cost $2. Non-members pay $4 for the first program per order and $2.50 for each additional program. Programs will be stacked on a cassette tape and mailed to you. PLEASE USE THE LIBRARY ORDER FORM.

ORDER FORM

ATLANTA 99/4A COMPUTER USERS' GROUP
P.O. BOX 19841
ATLANTA, GA 30325

PROGRAMS ORDERED:

	Program number	*Program name*
1.		
2.		
3.		
4.		
5.		
6.		
7.		
8.		
9.		
10.		
11.		
12.		
13.		
14.		
15.		

*TOTAL PROGRAMS ORDERED:*____ × *$2* = ______ + $1 = ______

NON-MEMBERS:____ × *$2.50* = ______ + $1.50 = ______

MAKE CHECK PAYABLE TO:
ATLANTA 99/4A COMPUTER USERS' GROUP

Your name: ____

Address: ____

City, State: ____

Zip Code: ______________

---

2. *EXCHANGE:* Persons that submit a useful, working program on cassette tape or disk may choose any three programs from this catalog for each program submitted. Submitted programs must be your original code, not copied from any source. You must complete the exchange form and sign the release statement for programs submitted or your entries cannot be accepted. The Users' Group reserves the right to refuse any program submitted due to errors or lack of usefulness. Your original tape or disk will be returned to you.

ATLANTA 99/4A COMPUTER USERS' GROUP
P.O. BOX 19841
ATLANTA, GA 30325

PROGRAM EXCHANGE FORM

Complete this form for programs submitted to the Users' Group as part of our software exchange policy. Submitted programs must be useful, error free, and your original code. You must sign the attached release statement or your programs cannot be accepted.

YOUR PROGRAM(S):

	Program Name	*Language* (Basic, XBasic, etc.)	*Requirements* (Speech, Joystk, etc.)
1.			
2.			
3.			
4.			

FREE PROGRAMS (Select three for each program above):

	Program Number	Program Name		Program Number	Program Name
1.			7.		
2.			8.		
3.			9.		
4.			10.		
5.			11.		
6.			12.		

RELEASE STATEMENT:

I ________________________________ certify that I am the sole author of the above program(s) and hereby give the Atlanta 99/4A Computer Users' Group permission to make minor modifications and enter the program(s) into their software library for duplication and distribution purposes. My only compensation will be my choice of any three programs listed in the Group's library for each of my programs submitted and accepted. I accept any and all consequences resulting from my misrepresentation and agree to hold the Users' Group harmless for any damages, monetary or otherwise, arising out of this transaction. I understand that I retain the authorship of the program(s) and may at any time, by written request, withdraw the same.

SIGNED:________________________________

Address:________________________________

City, State, Zip:________________________________

USERS'
GROUPS
TI

USERS' GROUPS

YOUR TI™ USERS' GROUP HAS LOTS TO OFFER

A TI™ Computer Users' Group is an organization of people who own TI computers. Their main purpose is to share information about TI-related programs and products, and to help each other expand the usefulness and enjoyment of their computing experience.

DO YOU NEED A USERS' GROUP?

Would you like to increase your software library with free public domain software?

Would you like to know where to find a commercial software package just right for your application?

Would you like to know what peripherals will work best with your TI computer?

Do you need help in hooking up the new hardware you've just bought?

Would you like to learn BASIC, Extended BASIC, LOGO, or Assembly language?

Do you have a program or idea that you'd like to share with other TI enthusiasts?

Would you like to work with others to develop software?

Would you like to get involved in community help projects?

Would you like to help your children learn from their computing experience?

Are you interested in computer telecommunications?

If you answered YES to any of these questions. . .you need a User's Group.

A User's Group can provide the solution to all of your computer-related questions. These questions represent only a small sampling of the wide range of service and support you can get from a TI™ Users' Group.

HOW CAN I FIND A LOCAL USERS' GROUP?

We've provided a State-by-State TI™ Users' Group listing, of the current clubs. (The list also includes clubs in Europe, Australia, and South America.) Browse through this list, find the club nearest you, then call or write.

The *99er Home Computer Magazine* and the *Enthusiast 99* also report on group activities. If you or a friend have access to a modem and TEXNET, you can see an updated list of users' groups and club news.

BUT, THERE'S NO CLUB NEAR ME!

If there isn't a club near you, or if the local club doesn't seem to fit your needs, you might consider starting a new Users' Group.

The key ingredients for a successful group are:

1) Five or more people who want to share information about their computers.

2) Two or more people willing to get things started.

STARTING A NEW USERS' GROUP

During your planning stages, it's a good idea to write to the people at the TI Users' Group Support Program or call Ed Wiest at 1-800-858-4565 and ask for their "Users' Group Starter Package".

Texas Instruments, Inc.
Attn: Ed Wiest, Users' Group Coordinator
P.O. Box 10508
Mail Station 5890
Lubbock, TX 79408-3508

The information we've provided here summarizes some of the material you'll receive.

FOUR IMPORTANT STEPS

1. Make contact with other computer users.

2. Announce your intention to start a Users' Group.

3. Hold your first meeting and keep meeting on a regular basis.

4. Ask for help, share ideas and stay informed.

1. MAKING CONTACT

Contact the nearest existing group and see if anyone there would like to join you, or knows of others who might. If there is no group of TI computer owners nearby, you'll have to develop your own contacts.

Retailers

Check in with local TI dealers, software stores, or general computer retailers in your area. Ask if they will:

1. Mail a notice to their customers for you, if you prepare it and pay for the postage.

2. Allow you to post a bulletin announcing your new group.

Schools and Colleges

Most schools and colleges have a newspaper, bulletin board, or public address system that will carry your message.

Local Companies

Contact the personnel director and ask to have your announcement circulated. Companies with engineering departments are likely to have computer hobbyists among their ranks.

Post Notices

Post notices on bulletin boards at the library, supermarket, and bank.

Use your modem

If you have a modem, you can post a bulletin on a number of local BBS's. (See our "Free Software By Phone" section for more information.)

Advertise

A small ad in your local newspaper can bring big results. Also, contact local radio and television stations and ask them if they'll run your announcement as a public service.

2. THE ANNOUNCEMENT

Be sure to include all the following information in your announcements:

> A NEW GROUP is forming for those owning, using or interested in the TI 99/4A HOME COMPUTER.
>
> FIRST MEETING: Date
> TIME:
> LOCATION: Address of the meeting
> PHONE: Please call (Name) at this number for further information or...come to our first meeting!

When you add your phone number to the notice, be sure to indicate the times you'll be available to chat...you don't want people calling you at any hour of the day or night.

3. MEETINGS

You should plan to hold meetings on a regular basis. Meetings can range from formal lectures to loosely moderated open discussions. It is always important to keep your meetings active, interesting and fun.

For many members, attending meetings will be their major form of participation. . . you must make sure that it's a rewarding experience for them.

Your first meeting

Make your first meeting an ACTIVE one. Most members will have just come from work and they'll want something INTERESTING!

Your first meeting should show your prospective members the value of your ACTIVE group. Demonstrations are the most convincing form of proof. You might invite an interesting speaker, demonstrate software, or show off an interesting project. You could also invite a local manufacturer to demonstrate an interesting software product or peripheral device.

Some things your new group can do

There are no set rules about what your group can or can't do. Most groups do some or all of the following:

HOLD MEETINGS
OFFER COURSES
PRESENT SPEAKERS
EVALUATE PRODUCTS
PUBLISH A NEWSLETTER
ANSWER MEMBERS' QUESTIONS
SHOW OFF MEMBERS' PROJECTS
MAINTAIN A SOFTWARE LIBRARY
PARTICIPATE IN COMPUTER CONFERENCES
ARRANGE GROUP PURCHASES AND DISCOUNTS

4. ASK FOR HELP

Ask for help from other Users' Groups. Share ideas and exchange information. Subscribe to other groups' newsletters...stay in touch...stay informed.

TI will help

TI's Users' Group Support Program can provide your club with valuable support.

TI will provide you with a "99/4A Home Computer Users' Group Start-Up Kit". The kit includes detailed instructions on setting up your Users' Group, conducting meetings, dealing with piracy and other problems; and it contains a constitution.

In addition, TI provides other services to users' groups. Club presidents can access a toll-free number for technical problems or queries that the consumer hotline can't answer. Says Ed Wiest of User Group Support, "We'll consult the experts to answer tough questions from club officers."

TI also sends users' groups new product announcements, similar to the information that distributors and dealers receive.

A valuable service that the clubs receive is free "Class B" software for group libraries. According to Ed, "Class B software is good, useful programs that are not marketable as commercial products."

"Users' Groups are the prime source of information on the TI 99/4A," states Ed Wiest. "Currently, there are more than 160 groups and we hear of three to five new groups forming almost every week!"

USERS' GROUPS

Mini-Profiles

We phoned TI Users' Groups across the country and around the world to gather profiles of typical and not-so-typical clubs. The response from *all* club presidents and officers was both enthusiastic and extremely helpful. Without their help this book would not be possible. THANK YOU!

We wanted to include profiles of all one-hundred-plus TI Users' Groups in *Free Software.* However, our schedule and the voluminous amount of data gathered would not permit us to do this.

We have profiled nine clubs (including England, Canada, and Australia) that demonstrate the spectrum of services and support you can expect to find as you explore the world of the TI Users' Groups.

These mini-profiles show you:

- where to get public domain software
- how to get help and advice on your hardware and programming problems
- how to get useful and informative newsletters and magazines
- how to find the Users' Group closest to where you live.

Wherever you are, there is probably a TI Users' Group near you!

Mini-Profile I

Atlanta 99/4A Computer Users' Group

"WE WANT PEOPLE TO REALLY UNDERSTAND WHAT THEIR TI COMPUTER CAN DO"

ADDRESS:

Atlanta 99/4A Computer Users' Group
Post Office Box 19841
Atlanta, GA 30325

OFFICER: Marshall Gordon, President
NEWSLETTER: *CALL Newsletter,* monthly
DUES: $15/year (individual or family rate)
MEMBERS: 250 locally, also through Southern United States
MEETINGS: Third Sunday every month at the Atlanta Public Library, 3 P.M.
ANSWERING SERVICE: (404) 926-6308

MEET ATLANTA'S 99ERS

Atlanta's active and growing TI Users' Group "wants to make computers comprehensible to everybody." The group offers a variety of support services to TI owners by phone, by mail, and in person at their monthly meetings.

FREE SOFTWARE

The Atlanta group is committed to offering a comprehensive library of user-contributed software. They now have more than 700 programs that span a variety of interests. Their business and professional offerings include "Investment Calculator" and two word processors. "Happy Spell" and "Name That Bone" are two of the entertaining educational programs available; there are many other programs in the game, music, utility, and home management categories.

Atlanta's library even includes several science/engineering programs like "Weather Station", which draws a professional station model based on the user's inputs.

All the programs in the software catalog can be purchased at a nominal fee that covers the cost of operation. Members pay $3.00 for the first program per order, and only $2.00 for each additional program. Non-members pay $4.00 for the first program in each order and $2.50 for each additional program. The programs are recorded on cassette tape and mailed.

Any individual that submits "a useful, working program on cassette tape or disk" can also choose any three programs for free for each program submitted—a nice motivation for program creators.

Atlanta's club officers are also aware of and concerned about the occasional "pirates" who try to take advantage of this great service. To protect the library and club members, all software contributors sign a release form stating that the program is theirs to contribute.

To encourage original contributions, the Atlanta group sponsors software contests for programs written in TI BASIC or Extended BASIC. Winners receive prizes of popular games, such as "Parsec" or "Golden Voyage."

"HANDS-ON" MEETINGS

TI 99/4A club members meet every month in a 300-seat meeting hall that offers acoustic facilities and a film screen. As many as 300 attendees fill the hall to learn about current happenings in the TI world and computer industry, lectures and descriptions of how to use LOGO, BASIC, and Extended BASIC, and hands-on demonstrations and evaluations of computer products, printers, and other equipment.

At a recent meeting the club hooked up TI computers to CompuServe for a hands-on demonstration of telecommunications.

SERVICES FOR OUT-OF-TOWNERS

Atlanta's TI 99ers are also concerned about members who can't attend meetings, because of geographical distance or physical disabilities. They offer two innovative services to members who can't be there in person.

- The club supports an answering service so members can call in with questions and problems. Their message is tape-recorded, and the person most able to answer their query calls back with a solution.

- The club is tape-recording their lecture demonstrations that teach TI owners how to program their machines and use them to their fullest advantage. "We plan to create courses on cassette, accompanied by notes, so that people who can't attend in person won't miss out on our classes."

The *CALL Newsletter,* which is included in the annual dues, provides useful information for TI owners everywhere. Recent issues featured software reviews, hardware evaluations, news on TI rebates and special club sales, and in-depth articles on programming. These include a series of detailed articles on how to write a data management program, assembly language programming, information on debugging, and helpful programming hints.

BEYOND COMPUTER LITERACY

The goal of the Atlanta TI group is to help TI owners go beyond computer literacy. "We want active members who will share their problems and solutions," says Marshall Gordon. "We would like everyone who is interested to learn to program and really enjoy all the capabilities of their TI home computer."

Mini-Profile II

99/4A Users of America, Flint, MI

"EXPLOIT THE POWER OF YOUR COMPUTER!"

ADDRESS:

99/4A Users of America
5028 Merit Drive
Flint, MI 48506

OFFICER: Duane B. Fischer, President
NEWSLETTER: *99/4 Users of America Newsletter,* every six weeks
DUES: $20/year (individual or family rate)
MEMBERS: 5,000 and growing, in the United States and Canada
MEETINGS: Monthly (except for summer) at University of Michigan campus, Flint, MI
ANSWERING SERVICE: (313) 736-3774

SHARING INFORMATION

The 99/4 Users of America are dedicated to sharing information, ideas, and services with TI owners in the United States and Canada. "We want, and need, your contributions, suggestions, and gripes," says club president Duane Fischer. "If we work together, we can have the most efficient and effective user group in the United States."

SUPPORT FOR HANDICAPPED USERS

In addition to meetings, special purchase plans, a programming hotline, and the many other services this group offers, the 99/4 Users of America also provide special support for handicapped computer owners.

The club's president manages mailings, the newsletter, coordination of activities, and some very sophisticated programming on his TI 99/4A—even though he is totally blind. Duane Fischer and other club members are using their ingenuity and TI home computers to develop computing aids to open up a new world to blind people.

Duane lost his sight eighteen years ago. "Friends tried to interest me in computers, but I couldn't see the screen! In 1980, my brother saw an ad for a home computer that also had a speech module—it was the TI 99/4. I bought one and fell in love with its speech capabilities."

Duane B. Fischer, President of 99/4A User's of America

Duane became so well acquainted with the computer's text to speech emulator, he discovered capabilities that Texas Instruments didn't know about! Duane uses the LIST"SPEECH" command to tell the computer to read out programs. He developed an "Error Reader" program that announces error messages to programmers who can't read them on the screen. He took advantage of the CRT's audio output to develop sound routines and audio cues that tell him exactly what's happening on the screen.

The club offers these programs to members, plus a "Talking Disk" catalog program, taped manuals and cassette reproduction of important technical material, and special prices for the Text to Speech emulator and other TI hardware and software.

Duane believes that there is a great market opportunity for software that utilizes the TI 99/4A's sound features. "Most handicapped people already have subnormal incomes," he says. "How can they pay the thousands of dollars necessary for Versa-Braille terminals or other specialized equipment? Every federal, state, and private agency in the United States would buy reasonably priced software for the TI 99/4A that converts text into speech. There is also a market for personal software such as checkbook management programs that utilize sound as well as graphics."

FREE SOFTWARE AND GOOD BUYS

The 99/4 Users of America have a public domain software library on both disk and cassette. Each member receives a program directory and five free programs. Additional programs can be purchased for only $2.00 each (with a minimum order of five programs per tape). Software is also available on disk for a slight additional charge.

The group is very careful about piracy and copyright infringement. "Some of us know what it's like to spend six months writing a program and then have someone steal it. We won't help pirates!" Duane says.

The group also sells TI software, hardware, and third-party software at 25% below suggested retail price. This service helps to support the club. Each member receives a 38-page directory of TI products with ratings and critiques. "Although we sell software and equipment, we won't sell advertising in our directory or newsletter. We want the freedom to evaluate products and give honest feedback and criticisms to our members."

Duane handles order entry and receipts for the mail order business with a combined sound/data base management program that he developed.

THREE-PART PROGRAMS

The 99/4 Users organize their monthly programs into three sessions. There is a one-hour tutorial on TI BASIC or other topics, demonstrations and critiques of products that emphasize how to use the product in ways that benefit the user, and a conference-style panel to answer questions. The club brings in full TI systems with monitors, drives, 48K memory, and other peripherals so they can answer any question that arises and demonstrate the solution.

The club also holds programming contests with hardware and software prizes and a monthly module drawing.

"We want to avoid cliques and stagnation at our meetings," Duane Fischer states. "Our emphasis is on sharing information so people can really benefit from their computers."

HELP FOR PROGRAMMERS

"You do not have to be a computer nut or professional programmer to be welcome among our ranks," Duane emphasizes. For those members who are interested in programming, the 99/4 Users of America offer several services. Members who can attend meetings can participate in the tutorials and panel discussions. The newsletter includes articles on programming and actual listings, as well as reviews of commercial software and equipment.

A really useful programming aid for members anywhere in the country is the group's Programming Hotline. If you have a programming problem you just can't solve, become a member and take advantage of this great service. The hotline operates from 2:00-4:30 P.M. Monday through Friday.

LOVE YOUR TI

"You have to be crazy or in love with your computer to run a users' group," says Duane Fischer. It takes a lot of love to provide services for everyone who uses the TI home computer, including handicapped owners.

Mini-Profile III

Winnipeg 99/4A Users' Group

"TI IN THE FAR NORTH"

ADDRESS:

Winnipeg 99/4A Users' Group
14 Stilwell Street
Winnipeg, Manitoba R2Y0M7
Canada

OFFICER: Gordon Bradshaw, President
NEWSLETTER: *Winnipeg 99/4 Users' Group Newsletter*
DUES: $10/year (individual or family rate)
MEMBERS: 40 families locally, also out-of towners.
MEETINGS: First Thursday every month (except July and August) in the Winnipeg Main Public Library

A LONG WAY FROM HOUSTON

"Winnipeg is straight north from Houston," says Gordon Bradshaw, "but it's a long way." When Gordon first bought his TI home computer, he felt like he was the only owner north of Texas. "I started looking for books on how to learn more about my TI. Finally, I found one other owner. We met at 7 P.M. one evening to talk and were still talking at 3 A.M." Gordon got some names of other TI users from a store and soon found himself president of a new TI users' group.

INTRODUCING PEOPLE TO THEIR TI

Ten people showed up at Winnipeg's first TI Users' Group meeting. Soon, word-of-mouth advertising began bringing fifty people to every meeting. "The majority," says Gordon, "are new computer users. Many are video game fans who thought that a computer would be better for their children than a game machine."

The Winnipeg group's goals are to "get people's feet wet—introduce them to their TI and learn what they can do with it."

Meetings emphasize tutorials and product reviews. Recently, the club rated game modules to help members in their software selections. The newsletter also offers book reviews, and the club has established a lending library. Because there is no local service or support for the TI, Winnipeg 99ers have to depend on their Users' Group, good books on programming, and their own ingenuity.

"Although Winnipeg is a large city, we're really out in the boonies and it's hard to get guest speakers. The Users' Group is really people's only resource around here to learn more about their TI computer."

GROWING SOFTWARE LIBRARY

Although the Winnipeg group is less than a year old, they now have a user-contributed software library of forty to fifty programs. "About half of the programs are games; the rest are divided between educational programs and business applications."

Members can buy programs on disk or cassette for only $2.00, and get three for free if they contribute a program. The Winnipeg group also pays contributors a small honorarium to encourage software development. "It's an incentive for the kids in our group to develop a program and earn a little money that can buy them some new hardware."

Like many other Users' Groups, Winnipeg's 99ers are strongly against software piracy. "If any member is found pirating another person's program, he will be asked to leave the group."

FROM SIX TO SIXTY

Winnipeg's membership spans a spectrum of ages, professions, and interests with one thing in common—enthusiasm for the TI home computer. "We have young kids and people in their sixties. All kinds of occupations are represented—from salesmen to garbage collectors to professionals."

One thing that concerns Gordon is that few women are currently participating. "We have family memberships and some teen-age girls are active in the group. But we'd like to find a way to reach the 'computer widows', too. My wife, for example, isn't especially interested in some of the hobbyist aspects of our TI, but she knows far more about word processing and other business applications than I do.''

Winnipeg's Users' Group even has a member in the Arctic Circle! ''Needless to say, he doesn't get to attend many meetings. But he receives our monthly newsletter and buys all our software.'' Which proves that you can probably form a TI Users' Group anywhere—even north of Houston.

Mini-Profile IV

Washington, D.C. Area 99/4A Users' Group

"I'D STILL BE IN THE DARK WITHOUT THIS GROUP"

ADDRESS:

Washington, D.C. Area 99/4A Users' Group
P.O. Box 267
Leesburg, VA 20075

OFFICER: Bill Whitmore, President
NEWSLETTER: *The Newsletter,* monthly, 28-32 pages
DUES: $12/year
MEMBERS: 850; affiliated groups in Maryland
MEETINGS: Second Thursday of each month at Fairfax High School auditorium, Fairfax, VA, 7 P.M.
PHONE: (703) 777-2017

FROM 8 TO 800

The Washington D.C. Area Users' Group has grown from eight members to 650 members locally, and over 150 additional members in sub-groups in Maryland, in less than two years.

Northern Virginia members meet in Fairfax, VA. Affiliated groups also get together in Williamsport, MD, and Montgomery County, MD.

Like any healthy adolescent, "we're working on ironing out our growing pains," says club president Bill Whitmore.

ACTIVE MEETINGS

The group works hard on creating varied and interesting meetings for their members. The Users' Group has organized lectures on TI hardware, including hands-on lessons about components and slides of the TI 99/4's "innards", lectures on "Efficient TI BASIC Programming", a talk on TI Writer and word processing; and is planning question/answer panel sessions.

Following the speaker, members break up into smaller groups for discussion, selling and swapping, and special interest groups.

"We're beginning to develop organized special interest groups," Bill says, "like the members who recently gave a presentation to the group on Assembly language programming."

The club has sponsored TI booths at area computer fairs and was responsible for demonstrations of TI LOGO, the Source, and the Peripheral Expansion Box.

FROM BEGINNERS TO PROFESSIONALS

According to Bill, the membership includes everyone from complete beginners to mainframe programmers. "Some of our members work with sophisticated mainframe systems daily. They bought the TI 99/4A in order to telecommute from home with the mainframe at their place of employment. We have members who are professional programmers and software developers; members who sell computers; and members who just want to learn more about their TI home computer and enjoy it."

The Washington D.C. group's active membership contributes to making their monthly newsletter a "mini-magazine". "We publish a 28-32 page newsletter," says Bill. "It's not just a leaflet—there is real content in this publication."

FREE SOFTWARE

The Washington D.C. Area Users' Group has accumulated a public domain software library of several hundred programs, both on disk and tape. Cassette users can now purchase twenty-seven tapes of free software programs. "Many members do buy all twenty-seven," states Bill.

Members can bring initialized disks with their name and phone number to meetings to have programs copied, or have cassettes duplicated by the Users' Group. Out-of-towners order by mail.

The price is an unbelievable $1 per cassette!

ELECTRONIC BULLETIN BOARD

TI users can also take advantage of the Washington, D.C. electronic bulletin board. Although the BBS does not have "downloading" capabilities, you can leave messages, exchange technical information and find solutions to your technical problems, and buy and sell equipment and software.

If you have a modem with your TI 99/4A system, give this BBS a call. Leave your name and address and within 24 hours you will get your own password to the system. Communicate by calling: (301) 681-5065.

INTERACT!

"We want to keep people interested and interacting, so they can learn the capabilities of their TI 99/4A and take advantage of it," says group president Bill Whitmore. "The TI home computer is superior because it's so easy to use—all it takes is a plug-in module to perform lots of sophisticated functions. I would still be sitting here in the dark without this group. Because of our TI Users' group, I've really learned a lot. We do all we can so every member can feel this way."

Mini-Profile V

The International 99/4A Users-Group

"THE LARGEST
COMPUTER USERS' GROUP IN THE WORLD!"

ADDRESS:

The International 99/4A Users-Group
P.O. Box 67
Bethany, OK 73008

OFFICER: Charles LaFara, President
NEWSLETTER: *Enthusiast '99,* monthly.
DUES: $12/year regular membership; President's Club membership $50/year
MEMBERS: 80,000 members worldwide!
PHONE: (405) 948-1023

WORLD'S LARGEST USERS' GROUP

Charles LaFara started the first TI Users' Group in August, 1980. The original club has grown from a starting membership of 946 to more than 80,000 people worldwide, including TI owners as far away as Saudi Arabia!

"We started originally out of sheer frustration," states president Charles LaFara. "We developed 25 simple programs, started trading, and the group and our software library grew and grew. . . and grew."

The International 99/4 Users' Group now combines several types of membership and services. The group has both a for-profit operation that sells equipment and software for the TI home computer PLUS a number of valuable support services and a huge public domain software library that are available for normal membership dues.

TWO KINDS OF MEMBERSHIPS

Regular members of the International 99/4 Users' Group pay $12 in annual dues. In exchange, the club offers them:

- discounted prices on all TI products plus third-party equipment and software (about 17% below suggested retail price)
- the *Enthusiast '99* magazine
- software catalogs
- call-in information and referral services
- software exchange library
- new product announcement bulletins

Special "President's Club" memberships are also available for $50 annual dues. President's Club members receive the same services as regular members. In adition, they are entitled to:

- a special cassette tape offer bimonthly (up to five free public domain software programs during the membership year)
- individually numbered membership card
- additional discounts on TI and third-party products from a special price list (about 9% above cost)
- President's Newsletter, bimonthly

According to the club, a President's Club membership is worth considering if you are planning to spend $150.00 or more for TI products over the next 12 months.

SOFTWARE EXCHANGE PROGRAM

The International 99/4 Users' Group has accumulated over 1200 user-written or translated programs for the TI 99/4, 99/2 and CC40. The programs include disk, cassette and hard copy.

Members can purchase programs on disk or cassette for only $3.00 each, including postage. (The minimum order is four programs.) Contributors who want to exchange their original programs for other public domain offerings can get any four programs for free from the catalog.

The software selection includes games, educational programs, business and professional programs, graphics, utilities, music, and even engineering programs.

EDUCATORS TAKE NOTE

The software exchange program is especially useful for parents and educators; selections feature math games and quizzes, bible study, spelling, geography, and music. President Charles LaFara states that at least 800 schools belong to the Software Exchange, which now offers more than 400 educational programs in TI BASIC and Extended BASIC.

SUPPORT SERVICES

The International 99/4 Users' Group employs fifteen full-time employees, including technical staff. "Our goal is to provide our members with technical expertise on the TI 99/4. Our staff can find the answer to any question."

Members can also call the Customer Assistance Hotline for problems with any public domain programs in the Software Exchange library. The Hotline is open weekdays from 8 A.M. to 4 P.M. Pacific Time. The Hotline's address and phone numbers are:

International Users-Group Library Services
116 Carl Street
San Francisco, CA 94117

(415) 753-1194

The *Enthusiast '99* magazine features program listings, software and equipment reviews, and tutorials (including a special column/tutorial for women).

The International Group also provides public domain programs to subscribers of TEXNET. TEXNET members can "download" programs via modem directly to their computers.

RAISING THE LEVEL OF COMPUTING

"We combine a profit-making operation (selling equipment and software) with completely free support services," Charles LaFara states. "Our goal is to benefit TI users in any way we can by raising their level of computing. We feel positive that we can maintain the level of interest in the TI 99/4. After all, there's an installed user base of more than one million units right now! We think the TI 99/4 is a great home computer."

Mini-Profile VI

The Daytona 99ers

"A FAST-MOVING GROUP"

ADDRESS:

Daytona 99ers
P.O. Box 4594
S. Daytona, FL 33581

OFFICER: Al Fox, President
NEWSLETTER: *The Daytona 99ers,* monthly
DUES: $12/year (individual or family rate)
MEMBERS: 119 locally, also out-of towners
MEETINGS: Third Thursday every month at 7 P.M., at the Daytona Beach Community College

STREAMLINED ACTIVITIES

It's no coincidence that the Daytona 99ers chose a speeding wheel as a symbol for their organization. This fast-moving Users' Group develops and organizes activities that will streamline any member's learning curve.

ORGANIZED MEETINGS

The group meets every month in a conference center at the Daytona Beach Community College. The center is equipped with a huge TV screen, which is hooked up to TI computers and a sound system for demonstrations. The meetings are organized to last about two hours and to provide activities for everyone from beginners to experienced users. "Typically, the hard-core people stay after the regular meeting to discuss special interests," explains club president Al Fox.

Each meeting starts with a review of club business, and demonstrations and discussions of commercial software. These can include game modules or business-oriented programs such as TI Writer and Multiplan. The Daytona 99ers have also given on-line demonstrations of The Source, TEXNET, and CompuServe.

The group then offers a "computer round table" for questions and answers, so experienced TI users can share their expertise with other members.

"Many of our members are complete beginners," Al says. "We try to reassure them that they and their questions are welcome. No query is too simple or too complicated—we just want to help."

The club also organizes teaching sessions during the meetings to offer tutorials on programming.

PROGRAM EXCHANGE LIBRARY

The Daytona 99ers have developed a software exchange library of more than 500 programs in TI BASIC, Extended BASIC, and Assembly language. "We want to encourage programming as well as purchasing," Al says. "Users who contribute original programs to the exchange get four programs for free."

The programs and catalog are available both to members and non-members. Members receive the catalog and updates with their annual dues; non-members pay $1.50 plus postage. The catalog is especially useful because it describes the memory and hardware requirements for each program.

For cassette programs, members pay only $1.50; non-members are charged $3.00. The club can copy up to 15 programs on each cassette, and can mail them to out-of-towners for only 75 cents postage. "We have some very good, useful programs in our library," Al says.

Members can also take advantage of the club's book and magazine lending library. "We also offer 'Teach Yourself BASIC' and cassettes on Extended BASIC, and loan members manuals and other technical information."

"THE BEST THERE IS"

"Our goal is to keep everyone excited and interested," states Al Fox. "We believe that the TI 99/4 is the best computer available in its price range. Lots of people buy it because they don't want to be left out of the Computer Revolution—but they really don't know what to do with it. Our role is to present the real benefits and applications of the TI computer to our members."

Another goal of the group is to encourage programming. "The programming languages available for the TI 99/4, such as LOGO and Extended BASIC, are some of TI's strong points."

The 99ers are open to every member's contributions. "We find that girls and women are equally active in our club," Al says. "Among the many active women members of the club are the 99ers' Secretary and a representative on the Steering Committee."

There is also lots of interest in the voice synthesizer, especially in relation to educational programs. "Speech tutorials are frequent items in our meetings, and we've assembled a good selection of public domain software that utilizes this feature to teach spelling, reading, and other subjects."

The Daytona 99ers intend to keep that wheel rolling as they get all their members up to speed on their TI home computers.

Mini-Profile VII

TIHOME

"TIDINGS FROM THE BRITISH ISLES"

ADDRESS:

TIHOME
157 Bishopsford Road
Morden, Surrey
SM46B8
England

OFFICER: Paul Dicks, President
NEWSLETTER: *Tidings,* six times yearly
DUES: 12 pounds/year
MEMBERS: 2,000+
PHONE: 0628 32839 and 0628 72448

BRINGING TI TO ENGLAND

Paul Dicks founded TIHOME "because I was the only person I knew who owned a TI." Although there are now twenty to thirty thousand TI owners in the British Isles, Paul's group is "virtually the only resource that TI owners have in England."

TI users face several obstacles, Paul explains. "Although the price of the TI home computer is reasonable, the government encourages the BBC Acorn and won't give schools subsidies to purchase TI 99/4 computers. Also, the price of peripherals is almost prohibitive—we're really working on trying to improve this situation. At this time, there are probably only 12 disk drive owners in the entire British Isles! Third-party software is just beginning to appear, but it's still difficult to even get a copy of *99er* magazine from any source other than our service."

To help British TI users, Paul founded a by-mail support group that offers services and helps TI owners contact others in their area to form local users' groups.

SOFTWARE AND SUPPORT

TIHOME offers members a resource for public domain software, some computer supplies, publications, local contacts, and technical information.

The software is catalogued by application, including games, graphics and demos, education, business, and utilities. Some of the offerings have a special flavor—such as "English Tennis".

The catalogue indicates what peripherals are necessary and how much memory the program uses. Members can order programs for 1 pound per program, or contribute a program and receive four for free.

TIDINGS

TIHOME publishes a 100-page magazine six times yearly, which members receive as part of their annual dues. The magazine offers editorials, comments, and advertisements by members; detailed software and book reviews; and in-depth tutorials and program listings. A recent issue features "Line Drawing Routine" as part of a discussion on TI Hi-Res graphics, reviews of TI Writer and game software, "Beginner's BASIC", tutorials on LOGO and Assembly Language, comments on computer shows and other activities, an in-depth article on concepting and programming adventure games, and reports from local users' groups all over the British Isles.

"The TI 99/4 is still the best-made computer in its price range, even in England," Paul comments. Despite the obstacles, true British pluck has paid off. TIHOME's membership went up from 180 to 2,000 in a year, and it's still growing!

Mini-Profile VIII

The Melbourne Users' Group

"TI DOWN UNDER"

ADDRESS:

TI 99/4A Melbourne Users' Group
59 Landstrom Quadrant
Kilsyth, Victoria
3173 Australia

OFFICER: Doug Thomas, National Coordinator
NEWSLETTER: *The Melbourne Users' Group Newsletter*

MAGAZINE: A group of Australian TI owners have started a new magazine on the level of *The 99er.* The new publication is an "all-Australian magazine, published exclusively for TI Computer Users." The subscription rate for *SOFTEX Magazine* is $25.00 for six issues. To subscribe to the magazine, or contribute articles and program listings, write to Doug Thomas for more details.

DUES: $10/year (Australian)
MEMBERS: 150 in Melbourne; six other groups in Australia
MEETINGS: Bimonthly in downtown Melbourne
PHONE: 725-8178

BRINGING TI TO AUSTRALIA

It took nine months for Doug Thomas to receive Extended BASIC for his TI 99/4—and he ordered it the same day he purchased his computer! There was obviously room for a resource closer to home for Australian TI owners. Doug is now National Coordinator for seven Australian groups and president of the Melbourne Users' Group.

"No one knew where to get software or information," Doug recalls. "Our other problem has been prices. Even with discounts and rebates, TI equipment is still quite expensive in Australia. We also pay a hefty import duty on software."

MEETINGS IN MELBOURNE

The Melbourne group meets every two months to share their enthusiasm and participate in activities.

The group originally emphasized hands-on demonstrations of hardware and applications. As members have become more sophisticated, the group is spending more time on discussions of debugging and programming techniques. Group meetings also include news reports on TI trends and products, and a question/answer period. "All the Australian Users' Groups have different personalities. Because Melbourne is a large city, many of our members are business-oriented professionals and the average age is from 30 to 50."

A group goal is to encourage special interest groups for businesspeople, ham radio hobbyists, and assembly language programmers. "There is also lots of interest in modems, which are especially relevant for a country as spread out as Australia. However, we again run into the problem of price—both for the equipment and services such as The Source. Members who belong to The Source pay $60-$70/hour to communicate with TEXNET or other services!"

Australian 99ers are looking forward to better supplies of the voice synthesizer. "There has been a shortage of this product in Australia. We're all very interested in its capabilities."

SOFTWARE EXCHANGE

Melbourne has assembled a software library of more than 300 programs. "At this point, most of our programs are games, but we also offer some music programs, and business applications such as a word processor."

Members can purchase cassettes for $5.50—a reasonable price for a tape that contains 15 programs!

The group exchanges software with other groups and sponsors software competitions to encourage more original contributions to the library. The Australian groups have jointly sponsored national competitions, with prizes donated by Texas Instruments. Prizes were given for beginner's programs, education programs, games, and programs for different configurations. All the contributions were donated to the Users' Groups' libraries.

KEEPING IN TOUCH

Obstacles aren't keeping TI users in Australia down. The groups exchange software, news, technical information and newsletters within Australia and with groups in England, California, Kentucky, and Oklahoma.

"Our goal is to disseminate as much information as we can on the TI home computer," Doug explains.

Mini-Profile IX

The Southern California Users' Group

"ENCOURAGING COMPUTER LITERACY"

ADDRESS:

The Southern California Computer Group
P.O. Box 2181
El Cajon, CA 92021

OFFICER: Chester Goward, President; George Holstein, Treasurer
NEWSLETTER: *The Computer Voice,* monthly
DUES: $15/year
MEMBERS: 90 members and growing
MEETINGS: Third Wednesday monthly at local community centers

A NEW GROUP FOR NEW TI OWNERS

"Most new TI owners are also completely new to computers," says George Holstein of the Southern California Computer Group. To help 99ers in Southern California, the El Cajon group was founded in March 1983. In only a few months, the group has grown to ninety members, publishes a newsletter, and organizes activities to bring computer literacy to Southern California.

CLASSES AND SPEAKERS

Each users' group meeting begins with an hour-long tutorial on topics such as TI BASIC, Extended BASIC, BASIC Hands-On Computer Literacy, and using sprites. The group also presents guest speakers to discuss trends in the computer world and demonstrate new products, such as TI-compatible joysticks.

The group has a Swap Meet table to enable members to exchange or sell equipment and software.

"Our goals are to promote computer literacy, develop a software cassette library, develop original programs, and provide information on TI-related products to our members."

GROWING SOFTWARE LIBRARY

The Southern California Group's software library is just getting started. In addition to acquiring public domain software and trading with other groups, "one of our most important goals is to develop our own user-contributed software."

Using the Speech Module and Extended BASIC, the group has developed a "raffle" program, which runs the monthly software raffle. At each meeting, the computer picks out the winning raffle ticket and announces the winner's name!

"We think that the 99/4's speech capability is really exciting," explains George. "For example, you can go on-line with a modem, Extended BASIC, and the Speech Module and tie into services like TEXNET or CompuServe. Once you're tied into a large computer system—such as a minicomputer or mainframe—your TI has an unlimited vocabulary and can read the news to you!"

A moving example of the power of TI's speech synthesizer was published in the May 1983 *Computer Voice.* One member wrote that the TI 99/4A and speech synthesizer was enabling her husband to re-learn speech, math, and reading abilities after a series of operations and a stroke. "I have only praise for the TI 99/4A. It has given Bill hope for re-learning the knowledge that was lost because of his afflictions."

THE COMPUTER VOICE

The Southern California Computer Group manages to pack a lot of useful information into a small newsletter. Each issue features TI and User Group news, "TI Tips" on products and programming, a "Query Corner", a "Computing Corner", and useful articles, such as "Interfacing the TI 99/4A with RS 232-compatible Equipment".

"We want to form a Super Users' Group," states one of the club's founders, Mike Brashars. "We want a group that provides a variety of dynamic demonstrations, tutorials, and activities—not only people socializing and waiting for something to happen."

It looks like the Southern California Computer Group is well on its way to making a dynamic contribution to area TI users.

TI 99/4A HOME COMPUTER USERS' GROUP LIST*

*Contact TI for the most recently updated list.

INTERNATIONAL GROUPS

The 99/4 Program Exchange
P.O. Box 3242
Torrance, CA 90510

99/4 Users of America
5028 Merit Drive
Flint, MI 48506
313-736-3774

New York 99/4A Users' Group
34 Maple Avenue
Armonk, NY 10504

International 99/4 Users' Group
P.O. Box 67
Bethany, OK 73008
405-948-1023

ALABAMA

Central Alabama 99/4 Users' Group
551 Larkwood Drive
Montgomery, AL 36109

Jasper 99/4A Users' Group
1F Northwood Townhome
Jasper, AL 35501

North Alabama 99 Computer
4126 Cherokee Drive
Huntsville, AL 25801

TIBUG
709 Nytol Circle
Birmingham, AL 35210

Wiregrass 99 Users' Group
106 Harwood Place
Enterprise, AL 36330

ARIZONA

Arizona 99 Users' Group
4328 E. LaPuenta Avenue
Phoenix, AZ 85004
602-841-8713

Southwest Ninety Niners Users' Group
6816 E. Lurlene Drive
Tucson, AZ 85730

Yuma 99er Users' Group
1573 E. Kuns Court
Yuma, AZ 85365

ARKANSAS

Artic K-Byters
Route Box 69
Van Buren, AR 72956

Little Rock 99er Users' Group
P.O. Box 55
North Little Rock, AR 72115

CALIFORNIA

Bechtel Employee's Computer Users
50 Beale Street P.O. Box 3965
San Francisco, CA 94119

Central Valley Users' Group
2419 Clemson Drive
Davis, CA 95616

Golden Gate Computer Users' Group
3617 Guerneville Road
Santa Rosa, CA 95401

Highway 99ers Computer Group
1277 East Avenue
Chico, CA 95926
916-343-4528

Kings 99/4A Users' Group
299 W. Birch
Hanford, CA 93230

LA 99er Computer Group
P.O. Box 3547
Gardena, CA 90247-7247

Orange County 99/4A Users' Group
3941 BS Bristol St., Suite 172
Santa Ana, CA 92704

Rancho Seco 99/4A
Home Computers Users' Group
Rancho Seco, 11440 Highway 104
Herald, CA 95638

South Bay 99er Users' Group
16380 E. LaChiquita
Los Gatos, CA 95030

San Gabriel Valley 99/4 Users' Group
1008 Dore Street
West Covina, CA 91712
213-330-8240

South California Computer Group
P.O. Box 21181
El Cajon, CA 92021

The Tri-Valley 99ers
306 Flittner Circle
Thousand Islands, CA 91360

COLORADO

Boulder 99/4A Users' Group
7129 Mt. Meeker Road
Longmount, CO 80501

Rocky Mountain 99ers
Box 3400
Littleton, CO 80161

DELAWARE

Delaware Valley Users' Group
25 Quartz Mill Road
Newark, DE 19711

Kent County 99/4A
Computer Users' Group
Box 354 Andrews Lake
Felton, DE 19943

FLORIDA

Brevard Users' Group (BUG)
P.O. Box 1402
Palm Bay, FL 32906-1402

Daytona 99ers
P.O. Box 4594
S. Dayton, FL 32021

Greater Orlando 99er Users' Group
P.O. Box 1381
Maitland, FL 32751

Manasota 99
6625 Roxbury Drive
Sarasota, FL 33581

Northwest Florida 99er
P.O. Box 3641
Pensacola, FL 32516

Penellas Peninsula 99/4 Users' Group
5060 86th Avenue N
Pinellas Park, FL 33565

South Florida 99 Users' Group
433 Wright Drive
Lake Worth, FL 33461

Tampa Bay 99er Users' Group
13097 Lois Avenue
Seminole, FL 33542

West Jax 99ers
7266 Bunion Drive
Jacksonville, FL 32222

GEORGIA

Atlanta 99/4A Computer Users' Group
P.O. Box 19841
Atlanta, GA 30325

Georgia 99/4A Users' Group, Ltd.
P.O. Box 88464
Dunwoody, GA 30356

Savannah Computer Users' Group
2723 Skidaway Road
Savannah, GA 31404

HAWAII

Aloha 99/4A Users' Group
92865 Palailai Street
Makakilo, HI 96706

ILLINOIS

Chicago 99/4A Users' Group
353 Park Drive
Palatine, IL 60067

East Central Illinois 99 Users' Group
3701 Tuttle
Danville, IL 61832

K:3 Users' Group
Route 2, Box 203
Momence, IL 60954

Lincolnland 99 Computer Group
P.O. Box 1434
Springfield, IL 62705

99/4A Owner Users' Group
8602 Dorr Road
Wonder Lake, IL 60097

INDIANA

Anderson 99er Users' Group
Route 2, Box 374-A
Pendleton, IN 46046

Hoosier Users' Group
P.O. Box 34334
Indianapolis, IN 46234-0334

Miami County Area 99/4A
Home Computer Users' Group
163 West Third
Peru, IN 46970

IOWA

Cedar Valley 99er Users' Group
2705 16th Avenue
Marion, IA 52302

Central Iowa 99/4A Users' Group
3013 E. 32nd Street
Des Moines, IA 50137

Northeast Iowa Home Computer
Users' Group
1421 Delta Drive
Cedar Falls, IA 50613

KANSAS

Mid America 99/4 Users' Group
P.O. Box 2505
Shawnee Mission, KS 66201

KENTUCKY

Kentuckiana 99/4 Computer Society
9801 Tiverton Way
Louisville, KY 40222

The Bluegrass Area
2210 Burton Park
Georgetown, KY 40324

LOUISIANA

Bayou 99 Users' Group
P.O. Box 921
Lake Charles, LA 70602

MAINE

Greater Sanford Users' Group
RFD 1, Box 275
Springvale, ME 04083

MARYLAND

Baltimore Users' Group
P.O. Box 3
Perry Hall, MD 21128

Severna Park 99/4A Users' Group
27 Whittier Parkway
Severna Park, MD 21146

MASSACHUSETTS

Club 99
34 Forest Street
Attleboro, MA 02703

Magnetic
57 River Road
Andover, MA 01810

MIT Lincoln Laboratory 99/4A
Users' Group
244 Wood Street
Lexington, MA 02173

M.U.N.C.H.
1241 Main Street
Worchester, MA 01603

New England 99ers
99 School Street
Weston, MA 02193

Personal Computer Users
P.O. Box 782
Westborough, MA 01581

Pioneer Valley 99/4 Users' Group
3 Market Street
Northampton, MA 01060

MICHIGAN

Central Michigan Computer 99
1970 Kibby Road
Jackson, MI 49230
517-784-4202

Grand Rapids 99 Users' Group
Box 1649
Grand Rapids, MI 49501

Home Computer Club
41599 Simcoe
Canton Township, MI 48188

Lower Michigan 99/4A Users' Group
18659 Lucy
Allen Park, MI 48101

MINNESOTA

MSP 99 Users' Group
P.O. Box 12351
St. Paul, MN 55112

MISSOURI

Jackson County 99ers
3012 Canterbury
Blue Springs, MO 64015

Kansas City 99/4A Computer Users
4511 N. Troost
Kansas City, MO 64116

Ozark 99er Users' Group
Route 1
Republic, MO 65738

99/4A Users' Group of St. Louis
271 Oak Pass Court
Ballwin, MO 63011

MONTANA

Big Sky 99ers Computer Users' Group
P.O. Box 1044
Great Falls, MT 59403

NEBRASKA

Crossroads 99'er Computer Group
511 Iowa Street
York, NE 68467

Lincoln 99 Computer Club
5401 S. 37th Street
Lincoln, NE 68516

NEW HAMPSHIRE

New Hampshire 99'ers Users' Group, Inc.
P.O. Box 7199, Heights Station
Concord, NH 03301

NEW JERSEY

Central Jersey 99/4A Users' Group
P.O. Box 673
Brick, NJ 08723

New JUG
Islean NJ Public Library
Green Street, NJ 08830

North Jersey 99er Group
52 Laura Avenue
Wanaque, NJ 07465

Northern NJ 99er Users' Group
P.O. Box 515
Bedminster, NJ 07921

SK 99 Users' Group
180 Haledon Avenue
Prospect Park, NJ 07508

9900 Users' Group
P.O. Box K
Moorsetown, NJ 08057

NEW MEXICO

Bernalillo 99/4A Home Computer
Users' Group
2008 Lead Avenue SE
Albuquerque, NM 87106

NEW YORK

Chautauqua County Users' Group
2209 Big Tree Road
Lakewood, NY 14750

R.G. and E.
71 Finnegan Way
Henrietta, NY 14620

Upstate New York 99/4 Users' Group
P.O. Box 13522
Albany, NY 12212

NORTH CAROLINA

Bits and Bytes Users' Group
139 Vance Street
Roanoke Rapids, NC 27870

Carolina 99/4A Users' Group
8467 Southard Road
Stokesdale, NC 27357

Charlotte 99 Users' Group
DOWD House at 2216 Momentum St.
Charlotte, NC 28202

Piedmont 99er Users' Group
316 Reynolds Drive
Statesville, NC 28677

The Forsyth 99er Computer Users' Group
4801 Selwyn Drive
Winston-Salem, NC 27104

OHIO

Cin-Day Users' Group
P.O. Box 519
West Chester, OH 45069-0519
513-777-0110

Cleveland Area 99/4A Computer Group
2385 Stanford Drive
Wickliffe, OH 44092

C.O.N.N.I.
1456 Grandview Avenue
Columbus, OH 43212

ECO 99er Users' Group
P.O. Box 1601
E. Canton, OH 44730

Summit 99er Users' Group
807 Washington Avenue
Cuyahoga Falls, OH 44221

OREGON

Pacific Northwest 99/4 Users' Group
P.O. Box 5537
Eugene, OR 97405

Portland Users of Ninety-Nines
P.O. Box 15037
Portland, OR 97215

Salem Oregon Ninety-Niner (SONN)
4981 Jones Road Street
Salem, OR 97302

Willamete Valley 99/4A Users' Group
740 SE Park Avenue
Corvallis, OR 97333

PENNSYLVANIA

Airport Area Computer Club
P.O. Box 710
Corapolis, PA 15108

Capitol Area Users' Group
P.O. Box 637 Federal Square Station
Harrisburg, PA 17108-9998

Central PA 99/4A Users' Group
(The Point) I-83 and Union Deposit
Harrisburg, PA 17109

Hazleton Area 99ers
P.O. Box 285
Hazelton, PA 18201

Lehigh Users' Group
P.O. Box 4837
Allentown, PA 18103

Meadville Area Computer Users' Group
RD #1, Box 274
Meadville, PA 16335

Philadelphia 99er Users' Group
552 Seville Street
Philadelphia, PA 19128

Pittsburgh Users' Group
P.O. Box 18124
Pittsburgh, PA 15236

RHODE ISLAND

Tri-State Users' Group
P.O. Box 457
Lincoln, RI 02864

SOUTH CAROLINA

Carolina Computer Club
225 Wynchwood Drive
Irmo, SC 29063

Piedmont 99ers Computer Group
P.O. Box 5921
Greenville, SC 29606

Sumter Computer Club 99ers
875 Bay Blossom Avenue
Sumter, SC 29150

TENNESSEE

Athens 99/4 Computer Users' Group
2215 Congress Parkway
Athens, TN 37303

Mid South Users' Group
8067 Neshoba
Germantown, TN 38138

Middle Tennessee Users' Group
P.O. Box 367
Estill Springs, TN 37330

TEXAS

Central Texas 99/4A Users' Group
P.O. Box 3026
Austin, TX 78764

Corpus Christi 99ers
3602 Braeburn
Corpus Christi, TX 78415

Dallas Home Computer Group
P.O. Box 672
Wylie, TX 75098

Houston Users' Group (HUG)
18103 Bambridge
Houston, TX 77090

JSC Users' Group (JUG)
2321 Coryell Street
League City, TX 77573

Lubbock Computer Club
3211 27th Street
Lubbock, TX 79410

Northeast Tarrant 99ers (NET)
P.O. Box 534
Hurst, TX 76053

San Antonio Area 99ers
P.O. Box 2509
Universal City, TX 78148

West Texas 99/4 Users' Group
P.O. Box 6448 M/S 3030
Midland, TX 79701

Young Peoples LOGO Association
1208 Hilldale Drive
Richardson, TX 75081

VIRGINIA

Southside 99/4A Computer Users' Group
356 Norwood Drive
Danville, VA 24540

Tidewater 99/4 Users' Group
942 Boiling Avenue #106
Norfolk, VA 23501

WASHINGTON, DC

Washington DC Users' Group
P.O. Box 267
Leesburg, VA 22075

WASHINGTON STATE

Puget Sound 99ers
P.O. Box 6073
Lynnwood, WA 98036

Western Washington Computer Club
10806 Kuhlman Road SE
Olympia, WA 98503

Tri-Cities 99er Computer Club
P.O. Box 1039
Richland, WA 99352

WISCONSIN

Fox Cities Users' Group
P.O. Box 2277
Appleton, WI 54913

Madison Area Home Computer
3518 Concord Avenue
Madison, WI 53704

Milwaukee Area Users' Group
2007 North 71st Street
Wauwatosa, WI 53213

Rock 99 Computer Club
Route 5, Box 399
Edgerton, WI 53534

Sheboygan Area Users' Group
P.O. Box 1151
Sheboygan, WI 53081

International

AUSTRALIA

Victoria Coordinator
59 Landstrom Quadrant
Kilsyth 3137
Victoria, Australia

New South Wales Coordinator
P.O. Box 101
Kings Cross 2011
New South Wales, Australia

Queensland Coordinator
127 Crowley Street
Queensland
Australia

Western Australia Coordinator
P.O. Box 246
Mt. Lawley 6014
Western Australia

South Australian Coordinator
26 Suffolk Avenue
Brahma Lodge 5109
South Australia

Tasmanian Coordinator
2 Binya Street
Glen Orchy 7010
Tasmania, Australia

Canberra Coordinator
69 Canopus Cresent
Girlang 2617
A.C.T., Australia

BELGIUM

Gebruikers Club Vlaanderen
Broekestraat 63
B-9670, Horebeke, Belgium

CANADA

Carleton Home Computer Users' Group
RR #2
Stittsville, Ontario
Canada K0A 3G0

Edmonton Users' Group
P.O. Box 11983
Edmonton, Alberta
Canada T5J 3L1

Karwartha 99er Users' Group
45-30 Champlain Cresent
Peterborough, Ontario
Canada K9L 1T1

Sudburry 99ers
2530 Ida Street
Sudburry, Ontario
Canada P3E 4X1

Toronto Home Computer Users' Group
3175 Kirwin Avenue, Townhouse #159
Mississauga, Ontario
Canada L5A 3M4

Vancouver Computer Users' Group
5825 Mayview Circle
Burnaby, BC
Canada Z5E 4B7

Victoria 99er Group
2602 Peatt Road
Victoria, BC
Canada V9B 3T8

Winnepeg Users' Group
14 Stillwell Street
Winnepeg, Manatoba
Canada R2Y 0M7

COLOMBIA

Associacion Columbiana
de Usuarios 99/4
Av Nutivara #C 3-6
Medellin Colombia SA

ENGLAND

TIHOME
157 Bishopsford Road
Morden Sury SM46BH
England

GERMANY

American Express International
Department 204
APONY 09757
Frankfort, Germany

Inquiries about Home Computer Users' Groups should be sent to TI, P.O. Box 10508, MS 5890, Lubbock, TX 79408, ATTN: Users' Group Coordinator.

FREE SOFTWARE BY PHONE

READ BEFORE DIALING

READ BEFORE DIALING

The MODEM (MOdulator/DEModulator)is an inexpensive device that allows you to use your TI computer to communicate with other computers through regular telephone lines. It has brought the age of telecommunications and FREE software within your reach.

As we were writing this book two very exciting events occurred in the world of TI telecommunications.

1. Texas Instruments Inc. introduced a low cost Direct Connect modem that allows you to get on-line *without* having to buy a Peripheral Expansion System.

2. The world's first TI Bulletin Board (T.I.B.B.S.) began operations. This new service is sure to spread across the country offering free TI public domain software by phone in the very near future.

A diverse network of services and recreations is now as close to you and your TI computer as your telephone. Hundreds of information services and electronic bulletin boards (BBS) are standing by at this moment waiting for you...and the ones you'll learn about in this book cost no more than the price of an ordinary phone call.

We will introduce you to the exciting new world of computer communications, so you can take advantage of these new developments.

IN THIS SECTION WE WILL SHOW YOU:

- The FREE services that are *now* available to you, and a glimpse into the future.

- A review of the outstanding services provided by TEXNET Information Service, including their extensive library of free public domain software.

- MODEM terms fully explained.

- A complete MODEM buyer's guide including brands, features

and cost...PLUS, the names and addresses of major MODEM manufacturers.

- Special recreational systems like the "Living Tree" and "DIAL-YOUR-MATCH" are fully covered.

- A comprehensive phone directory of over 500 numbers that puts you in touch TODAY, with BBS and recreational systems.

- How to set up your own BBS. Featuring an exciting interview with the founder of T.I.B.B.S.

Free Bulletin Board Services (BBS)

Users' Groups, hobbyists and entrepreneurs throughout the world are operating electronic Bulletin Boards and information terminals. These are loaded with easy-to-access features that allow you to expand the usefulness of your computer.

The FREE Electronic Classified Ad

The Message Center is the heart of each electronic Bulletin Board. Do you have information to share with other TI enthusiasts? Something to sell? Looking for some programming help or some new or used equipment? You'll probably find what you want listed in the "computer classified ad department": the electronic Message Center.

Later in this section you'll learn how to retrieve and place messages on a wide selection of electronic bulletin boards. Here's what a typical message looks like:

```
MSG#0326 DATE: 02/02/83 TIME:18:26:49
FROM: Mary Dillon; Cupertino, CA Educators
TO: All
SUBJ: Classroom reading programs

Looking for (TI) reading skills programs for 1st grade
Students. Please leave message on this BBS if you can help.
```

Using this FREE service offers many exciting possibilities. . . You can advertise a product or service, find out the latest TI news, or leave a message for a friend.

COMING SOON:
FREE Public Domain Software

Public domain software is either uncopyrighted software that has been contributed by a fellow TI enthusiast, or copyrighted software that has been put on a BBS with the author's approval.

With the advent of the first TI Bulletin Board, you'll soon be able to call TI BBS, check its list of available software, and *download** public domain programs to your own computer, adding them to *your* software library.

All types of programs will soon be available: utility programs that ease your programming chores, adventure and arcade games, educational software, business software, communications software, home management software. *There is now a program available that allows you to set up your own BBS!*

AN EXAMPLE OF PUBLIC DOMAIN SOFTWARE ON A BBS

Your TI Home Computer and Modem allow you to contact any BBS in the world by telephone. Of course, you can only download programs from Bulletin Boards that have TI software in their libraries. The TI BBS network is just beginning to catch on across the country. (See page 117.) To show you what will soon be available, we contacted a non-TI BBS in Washington, D.C., and "asked" what software was available there. We were presented with this menu:

---

* *Download: To receive a program over the phone line, temporarily capture it in your TI's memory, then permanently save it on cassette or disk for later use.*

1. Communications-related
2. Utilities
3. Games
4. Other
5. User-submitted
6. New text
7. VisiCalc
8. Forth
9. New

To see what Utility programs were available, we pressed "2" [ENTER] and were presented with this screen:

#	File Name	SIZ	#	File Name	SIZ
1:	DISKDUP	007	2:	DISKPEEK	019
3:	DISKRPM2	007	4:	DSKTOCAS	016
5:	MAILABEL	007	6:	NEATLIST	016
7:	SCRNDUMP	005	8:	SETAUTO	009
9:	SETAUTO2	012			

Many BBS's provide a description of each program so you don't have to decipher the shortened program names, and are able to download only the programs you are interested in.

Some BBS's offer "computer posters", graphic designs and portraits of famous people like Albert Einstein and Raquel Welch. These posters can be printed out using a standard printer, then displayed proudly on the wall of your computer room.

One BBS offers programs in Basic, posters, text and VisiCalc files, and Ham Radio information. The software available covers the spectrum from games like BLASTER, to educational programs like TYPER, a typing tutorial.

A complete word processing program can be downloaded from some BBS's. Soon you will be writing the great American novel on your computer—using FREE software!

GOOD NEWS FOR TI COMPUTER OWNERS

With the advent of T.I.B.B.S., FREE software by phone is now on its way to TI owners. You may even be one of the people who will make it possible!

WHAT'S NOW AVAILABLE FOR TI OWNERS:

When you call a BBS, you can also get an updated listing of other BBS's; talk, via the keyboard to the SYSOP (System Operator); *Upload** your programs to the system; get the current time and date; or take part in a BBS experiment. One BBS offers its callers a short quiz, and awards prizes for the correct answers.

The BBS network has software and features for every TI computer owner. It's all FREE, and as close as your telephone! *This section will show you where it is and how to get it.*

Other Free Services

Once you've been bitten by the "computer communications bug" you'll discover many new and interesting recreations and services.

THE LIVING TREE

Later we'll show you how to access and actively participate in the growth of a "Living Tree" system.

As its name implies, a "Living Tree" service is a vast and *ever-expanding information bank* structured like a living tree. After making contact with your local "Living Tree" you enter the system's data base at its "top". By inputting commands like "down", "up", "left" or "right", you slide down its "trunk" or climb onto its various "limbs" and "branches".

Personal Mail Boxes reside in one branch of the tree, Classified Ads in another, and a "Living Story" in yet another.

**Upload: To send a program from your TI computer to a distant computer via phone lines.*

In the "Living Story", you'll be able to contribute your own continuation to the existing narrative. If you're a budding writer, this may be your chance to show your literary talents. Many youngsters who participate in this activity have measurably improved their writing and reading skills while using their creative talents.

Most "Living Trees" don't offer free software, but they do give you the opportunity to add to their ever-expanding structure and access lots of valuable information.

DIAL-YOUR-MATCH

DIAL-YOUR-MATCH is another good example of the many FREE services available to TI communicators. This confidential "find-a-mate by modem" service is available FREE in more than 15 locations throughout the U.S. You enter a code name, answer a brief questionnaire, and check back periodically to see if you've been matched with the romance of your life.

A complete phone directory of *all* available DIAL-YOUR-MATCH terminals can be found on page 133.

THE LIST IS GROWING

The list of FREE services available to TI computer owners is growing daily. Entering this exciting world is as easy as buying a modem, hooking it up, and dialing your phone.

READ ON!

Read on, and learn how you can enter this exciting world of computer communications.

Downloading a Program from Another TI Computer or TEXNET

FIVE EASY STEPS TO FREE SOFTWARE

1. Call up another TI Computer or TEXNET.
2. Look over their files and choose the public domain program you'd like to download.
3. "Tell" the other computer to send the program to your computer's (RAM) memory.
4. Store the program on your disk or tape.
5. You have now added a new program to your permanent software library. . .ENJOY!

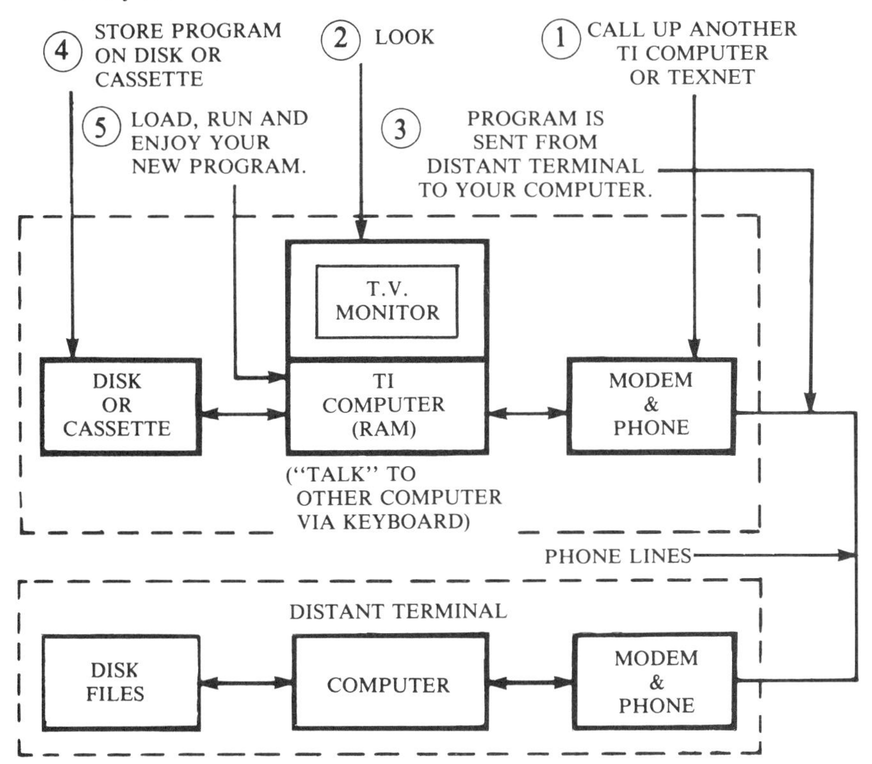

Uploading a Program to Another TI Computer or TEXNET

SHARING YOUR PROGRAM WITH OTHER TI ENTHUSIASTS

1. Place the disk with your program in the disk drive, or your cassette in your tape recorder. When the computer is ready to send your program, it will automatically read the disk or tape.

2. Call up TEXNET or another TI computer terminal and "ask" to upload your program.

3. Send your program.

   Your program is added to the public domain software file for use by other TI enthusiasts.

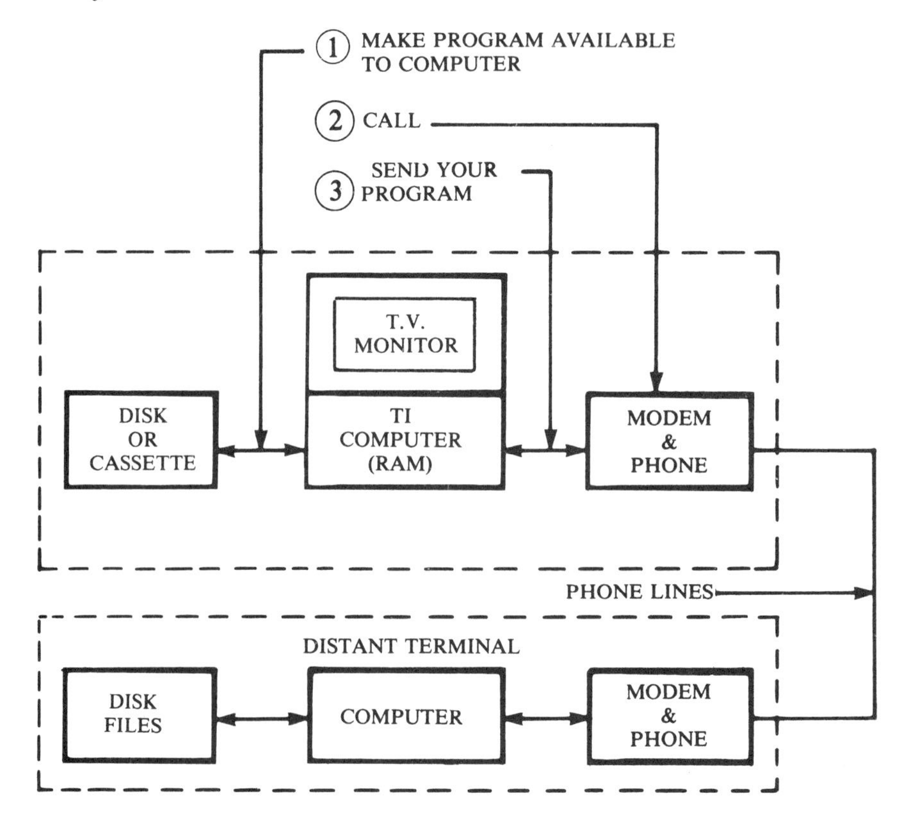

MODEMS

Now that you have an idea of all the FREE services and recreations available to TI communicators, it's time to start thinking about buying a MODEM. Before you run down to your local computer store, take a few minutes to read this short chapter. It will familiarize you with MODEM telecommunications terms and help you select the *right* MODEM for your needs.

Modem Terms & Features

MODEM

"MODEM" is the abbreviated combination of the two words MOdulator and DEModulator, (Modulator = Transmit and Demodulator = Receive).

A MODEM is used to interface between your computer and a telephone line. It enables your computer to communicate with other computers.

ACOUSTIC or DIRECT-CONNECT?

When you're shopping for a Modem you'll be presented with two basic choices; an acoustically-coupled modem or a direct-connect type.

ACOUSTIC MODEM

An acoustic modem is equipped with two soft rubber cups that accept a telephone's handset and form a tight seal around both the mouthpiece and earpiece. This type of modem can only be used with "standard" business type telephones. Fancy phones with odd shaped mouth and earpieces, like the "Princess" model, won't fit securely into the specially designed rubber cups. A tight, sound proof fit between telephone and modem is critical for proper operation... extraneous noise can distort the data transmission.

Acoustic modems are generally less expensive than direct-connect modems and are quite suitable for Up and Downloading information to your computer. (We've used the TI Telephone Modem, model PHP1600C acoustic modem to do the research for this book.) However, acoustic modems do not have the ability to automatically answer the phone, and are therefore not suitable if you want to start your own BBS.

To use an acoustic modem you pick up the phone, dial a BBS number, listen for the answering tone, and insert the phone's headset into the two rubber cups to establish contact.

DIRECT-CONNECT MODEM

Auto-Answer

A direct-connect modem plugs directly into a telephone wall jack. This eliminates any possible noise problems and allows for the "automatic answer" feature, necessary for operating your own BBS. Make sure that your home is equipped with a modular phone jack, since you'll probably need this for connection.

A phone is usually plugged into a modular wall-jack *with* the direct-connect modem via an inexpensive "Y" jack. (You can purchase a "Y" jack at any phone store and at most department stores.) This dual hookup lets you manually dial up the BBS or service of your choice. When connection is made you will hear a tone, an indicator will light on the modem, and communications can begin.

Automatic Dialing

Some direct-connect modems offer an automatic dialing feature. You can store commonly called phone numbers in the modem's terminal software. When you turn on your system, your screen displays a menu listing of these BBS's or services. By typing the number to the left of a listing, the modem will automatically dial the phone number of your choice. Here's what a typical autodial menu list might look like:

```
          AUTODIAL

     1. I.B.B.B.S.
     2. G.F.X.B.B.S.
     3. DATA BANK
     4. S.C.B.B.S
     5. STUART-S'VALE
     6. SANTA CLARA PMS
     7. TEXNET

           SELECT
```

Data/Voice Switch

In most direct-connect modems you can select either Data or Voice operation by pressing a switch.

The Data position lets you automatically dial out.

The Voice selection allows you to dial a number manually.

Other Options

Other options available on some direct-connect modems include automatic disconnect, and unattended automatic dialing and passing of data with other systems.

BAUD RATE

A baud rate is simply a measure of how fast a modem communicates. *All the BBS services available to TI computer owners operate at 300 Baud.* This translates to a rate of 30 characters per second.

Modems are also available that are capable of transmitting and receiving at 1200 Baud, (120 characters per second), or even faster. You might consider one of these faster units *if* you are planning to do *a lot of communicating* with commercial main frame computer networks such as TEXNET. One current drawback to this cost-saving option is that TI's Terminal Emulator II software package will only accommodate up to 300 Baud. New software is being developed at this time that will overcome this obstacle.

The faster the baud rate, the higher the cost of the MODEM.

DUPLEXING

Most modems have the switchable ability to operate either in full-duplex or half-duplex mode.

Full-Duplex

Full-duplex communication is similar to a telephone conversation, where both parties can talk simultaneously.

When you contact a BBS, make sure that the "Duplex" switch is set to "Full". The BBS will echo the characters you've sent back to your computer for display on your screen as it receives your information. This requires full-duplex operation.

Half-Duplex

Half-duplex can be compared to Ham radio communications, where only one party can talk at a time.

EXTRA FEATURES

Self-test

A test switch is provided on some modems that allows you to determine if your system is functioning correctly or if there is a problem at the other end of the connection.

Carrier Detection

When you make contact with another computer it responds by transmitting a carrier tone. Most modems let you know that you're in contact by emitting a tone or turning on a light.

Helpful Modem Buying Tips

TI manufactures two excellent modems: an acoustic model and a new direct connect modem. The "TI Modem Buyer's Guide" on page 99 lists TI-compatible modems produced by other manufacturers. It has been designed to give you an overview of each manufacturer's product(s), and an idea of each modem's cost. There are, however, a few additional considerations.

Do I need a Peripheral Expansion System?

Most modems will only work when used with the TI Peripheral Expansion System equipped with an RS-232 Interface card. If you have this equipment you're all set. *Your modem plugs into the rear of the RS-232 Interface Module.*

TI 99/4A with Peripheral Expansion System

But, I don't own a Peripheral Expansion System!

If you don't own a Peripheral Expansion System and an RS-232 Interface, buying these two units might cost you more than the modem. Fortunately, you can now add a modem to your TI-99/4A without having to purchase an Expansion box.

TI's New Telephone Modem

TI has just announced the release of their new direct-connect Telephone Modem. This 300 Baud full-duplex unit will reportedly retail for $99.00. It plugs into a small module called the "HEX-BUS Interface" that plugs neatly into the expansion port on the right of the computer. The HEX-BUS Interface will retail for approximately $50.00, making your total investment for both modem and interface less than $150.00.

A.J. International's RS-232 Controller

If you'd like to add other manufacturers' modems and RS-232 compatible peripherals to your TI-99/4A, you might consider the RS-232 Controller manufactured by A.J. International, 4023 Sommers Avenue, Drexel Hill, PA 19026, (215/623-8083). This RS-232 interface unit also does away with the Peripheral Expansion box and at $169.00 (including user's manual) will support *any* RS-232 compatible modem.

What About Terminal Software?

TI's Terminal Emulator II

Terminal software is needed to turn your computer into a communications terminal.

At this time there is only one terminal software package available: TI's Terminal Emulator II. Terminal Emulator II allows you to communicate with remote computer systems, like The Source, or with other TI home computers. The software comes in module form and plugs directly into the cartridge slot.

The next section, (after we present the Modem Buyer's Guide), will help you get started using the Terminal Emulator software module. After you become familiar with it you will find that Terminal Emulator II features provision for Auto Log-on, used to automatically log you on to a commercial computer system. More importantly, it allows you to upload or download valuable programs to and from similarly equipped computers. Coupled with TI's Speech Synthesizer, the Terminal Emulator "reads" text aloud as it appears on your computer's screen. Imagine having the news read to you while you drink your morning cup of coffee!

More Terminal Software is on the Horizon

Mr. Ralph Fowler of Lobo Inc., Kennesaw, Georgia is now writing terminal software for the TI-99/4A. Read our interview with Ralph on page 117 to learn about this innovative man and how his exciting projects will help you get free software by phone.

Cables and Connectors

Before you leave the store with your new modem, make sure that it comes supplied with all the correct cables and connectors. It could be extremely frustrating to get home with your modem and find that you've got the wrong cables!

Cables used to connect other manufacturers' modems (other than TI) to the RS-232 interface card must use an *EIA RS-232C 25-pin male connector.* Appendix B of Texas Instruments' RS-232 Interface Card Manual contains a helpful chart that you can refer to if you're in doubt.

Talk to the Manufacturer

Below is a listing of modem manufacturers whose products are summarized in our "TI Modem Buyers Guide". Additional manufacturers of interest to TI computer owners are also listed.

It's a good idea to send each manufacturer a short letter requesting information on their line of TI modems. Ask them to send you their brochures, then sit back in the comfort of your home and make your selection. You might also ask where their nearest distributor or retail outlet is; this can save you a lot of leg work. All the manufacturers we spoke to were extremely helpful and responded with literature within a few days.

Modem Manufacturers Listed in the TI Modem Buyer's Guide

Hayes Microcomputer Products, Inc.
5923 Peachtree Industrial Blvd.
Norcross, GA 30092
404-449-8791

The Microperipheral Corporation
2643 151st Place N.E.
Redmond, WA 98052
206-881-7544

Novation, Inc.
18664 Oxnard Street
Tarzana, CA 91356
213-996-5060

Prentice Corporation
266 Caspian Drive
Sunnyvale, CA 94086
408-734-9810

Racal-Vadic
222 Caspian Drive
Sunnyvale, CA 94086
408-744-0810

Universal Data Systems
5000 Bradford Drive
Huntsville, AL 35805
205-837-8100

More Modem Manufacturers

Anderson Jacobson, Inc.
227 Devcon Drive
San Jose, CA 95112

ESI Lynx
123 Locust Street
Lancaster, PA 17602

Kesa Company
774 San Miquel Avenue
Sunnyvale, CA 94086

Lexicon Corporation
1541 N.W. 65th Avenue
Ft. Lauderdale, FL 33313

MFJ Enterprises, Inc.
921 Louisville Road
Starkville, MS 39759

Micromint, Inc.
917 Midway
Woodmere, NY 11598

TRW Corporation
Modem Department
3444 Hancock Street
San Diego, CA 92110

U.S. Robotics, Inc.
1035 West Lake
Chicago, IL 60601

TI MODEM BUYERS GUIDE

	TI	*Hayes*	*Hayes*	*The Microperipheral Corp.*	*The Microperipheral Corp.*
Model:	830	Smart Modem 300	Smart Modem 1200	A1	A1A
Type:	Acoustic	Direct Connect	Direct Connect	Direct Connect	Direct Connect
Compatability	RS-232C	RS-232C	RS-232C	RS-232C	RS-232C 850 Int required
Baud Rate	300	0-300	0-300/ 1200	300	300
Duplex	Both Switch	Both Switch	Both Switch	Both	Both
Voice/ Data Selection	N/A	No	No	Yes	Yes
Auto Answer	N/A	Yes	Yes	No	Yes
Auto Dial	N/A	Yes	Yes	No	Yes
Self Test	No	Yes	Yes	No	No
Carrier Detection	Light	LED	LED	LED	LED
Cables & Connector Included?	Yes	No	No	Yes	Yes
Terminal Software Included?	No	No	No	Yes	Yes
Warranty	90 days	2 years	2 years	90 days	90 days
*Price	$199.95	289.00	$699.00	$199.00	$239.00

TI MODEM BUYERS GUIDE

	Novation	*Novation*	*Novation*	*Prentice Corp.*	*Prentice Corp.*	*Prentice Corp.*
Model:	J-CAT	103	103/212	STAR	P212	212TCM
Type:	Direct Connect	Direct Connect	Direct Connect	Acoustic	Direct Connect	Direct Connect
Compat-ability	RS-232C	RS-232C	RS-232C	RS-232C	RS-232C	RS-232C
Baud Rate	0-300	0-300	300/ 1200	0-300	0-300/ 1200	0-300/ 1200
Duplex	Full Only	Full Only	Full Only	Both Switch	Both	Both
Voice/ Data Selection	No	Yes	Yes	N/A	Yes	Yes
Auto Answer	Yes	Yes	Yes	N/A	Yes	Yes
Auto Dial	Yes	Yes	Yes	N/A	No	Yes
Self Test	Yes	Yes	Yes	Yes	Yes	Yes
Carrier Detection	LED	LED	LED	LED	LED	LED
Cables & Connector Included?	Yes	Yes Except RS-232	Yes Except RS-232	No	No	No
Warranty	1 year	1 year	1 year	1 year	1 year	1 year
*Price	$149.00	$249.00	$595.00	$199.00	$695.00	$795.00

TI MODEM BUYERS GUIDE

	Racal-Vadic	*Racal-Vadic*	*Racal-Vadic*	*Universal Data Systems*	*Universal Data Systems*	*Universal Data Systems*
Model:	VA103	VA212LC	VA212PA	103JLP	212A	212A/D
Type:	Direct Connect	Direct Connect	Direct Connect	Direct Connect	Direct Connect	Direct Connect
Compat-ability	RS-232C	RS-232C	RS-232C	RS-232C	RS-232C	RS-232C
Baud Rate	0-300	0-300/ 1200	0-300/ 1200	0-300	0-300/ 1200	0-300/ 1200
Duplex	Full Only	Full Only	Full Only	Full Only	Full Only	Full Only
Voice/ Data Selection	Built In	Yes	Yes	Yes	Yes	Yes
Auto Answer	Optional	Yes	Yes	Yes	Yes	Yes
Auto Dial	Yes Optional	Manual Only	Yes	No	No	Yes
Self Test	No	Yes	Yes	No	Yes	Yes
Carrier Detection	Tone	Light	Light	LED	LED	LED
Cables & Connector Included?	No	No	No	No	No	No
Warranty	1 year	1 year	1 year	1 year	1 year	1 year
*Price	$250-380	550.00	$795.00	$195.00	$675.00	$745.00
Special	This modem is built into a phone. Touch-tone or dial opt.					

N/A: Not applicable

*Price: Manufacturers recommended retail price. 5/15/83

TERMINAL SOFTWARE FOR YOUR TI

Congratulations. . .You have a modem, it's hooked up to your TI computer, and you're ready to call up a friendly BBS and get going! But, you need TERMINAL SOFTWARE to turn your TI into a communications terminal.

Right now, that means buying the Terminal Emulator II™ command module from Texas Instruments. However, other companies will soon start making alternative terminal software. Some generous programmer may even write his or her own terminal program and donate it to the public domain. Check with your local Users' Group to find out whether FREE public domain terminal software is available.

Since you will probably be using TI's Terminal Emulator II, we've included some instructions for it. We don't have space to tell you *everything* about it, so be sure to also read the manual that comes with the plug-in module! This section should smooth your way, and help you get started with this new way of communicating. In a few more pages we'll give examples of *real telephone conversations* with computer Bulletin Board Services.

Getting Started

Before you can call a BBS, you naturally need to know the telephone number to call! You might try the T.I.B.B.S. (p. 117), or you can look for a local phone number in the Directory on page 134. Of course, if you call a long-distance phone number, the phone company will charge you for it. THAT'S not free!

Be sure you have all your equipment plugged together properly, and turn it on in the right order, starting with the peripherals, then the Peripheral Expansion Box (if you have one), and last of all, your TI computer. You should have your telephone connection handy, but you don't have to connect the TI to the telephone yet.

It is a good idea to have the SHIFT LOCK key on your TI in the down position, because some BBS's can't receive lower-case letters properly. Stick with upper-case until you are more experienced.

The Terminal Emulator plug-in module works the same way as any of TI's "solid state software": When you plug in the module, then turn on the computer and type any key, you get a master selection list. At this point you may, if you wish, choose *"Default Option TE II"*. However, you'll get better results if you select *"Terminal Emulator II"*, and then do the following steps:

When you choose *"Terminal Emulator II"*, the "COMMUNICATION SETUP" display will appear on the screen.

COMMUNICATION SETUP

PARAMETER	OPTIONS	CHOICE
BAUD RATE	1 — 300	1
	2 — 110	
PARITY	1 — EVEN	1
	2 — ODD	
	3 — NONE	
DUPLEX	1 — FULL	1
	2 — HALF	
RS-232 PORT	1 — #1	1
	2 — #2	
COLUMN WIDTH	1 — 40	1
	2 — 38	
	3 — 36	
	4 — 34	
AUTO LOG-ON	FILE = LOGON	

Press the ENTER key four times and the cursor will move down past the first four Setup Choices. They are okay for most BBS's and we won't want to change them. However, the fifth choice, "COLUMN WIDTH", needs to be changed. Right now it is set at Choice 1: 40 columns. Your TI can handle 40 columns across the TV screen just fine, but most TV's and monitors *can't*. You'll probably lose one or two characters on both the left and the right end of each line of print on the TV screen. This is a nuisance, so let's change it to Choice 3: 36

columns. While the cursor is sitting on top of the blinking number "1", type the "3" key. The one will change to a three.

Now press ENTER once, and the cursor will be sitting on the last item in the Setup Choice list. Right now, you have no LOGON file and you don't want to use the "AUTO LOG-ON" choice. Erase the file name "LOGON" by typing several spaces. Now you are ready to use your equipment to contact a BBS. Press ENTER again.

If you chose the *"Default Option TE II",* or if you made your own choices, you should now have a white screen with the cursor sitting up in the top left corner. You might want to turn down the brightness on the TV monitor, since the white is much brighter than a blue background. Now dial the phone number for the BBS of your choice, listen for a high-pitched tone, and connect your computer to the telephone. With an acoustic modem, place the phone handset in the modem cradle. With a direct-connect, plug the modem cord in properly. Press the ENTER key two or three times, and you should be in touch!

We've found that "diving right in" is the best way to get comfortable with this new way of communicating. Don't worry about making mistakes while you are on-line with another computer. . . *IT'S ONLY A MACHINE!* You can't hurt it, and it can't hurt you!

From this point on, just try to "talk" to the BBS. Answer its questions, and when it gives you the chance try giving it a command. After playing with it for a while, you might want to read the next chapter of this book , through p. 148. It gives examples of conversations with BBS's, and discusses some typical situations.

Whenever you are done using a BBS, be sure to hang up the telephone. Most BBS's can only receive one telephone call at a time, so if you don't hang up then no one else can enjoy using the message system.

Special Commands

What do you do if you make a typing mistake on your TI? Normally, you'd press the FCTN S key, the ←. However, when you are in contact with a BBS, this usually won't work. It isn't enough to make *your* computer fix the mistake, you have to tell the *other* computer also! To do this, press a CTRL H. On most BBS's, this is a "BACKSPACE" command. If CTRL H doesn't work, try FCTN V, which is a "DELETE" command. This also usually works, but it gives a very funny-looking display.

Sometimes the BBS will start sending a very long message to your TI, a message so long that it starts scrolling off the top of the TV screen. On most BBS's, you can make the message pause so you can read it, by pressing a CTRL S. When you have "caught up", you can make the message continue by pressing CTRL Q.

Your TI computer "remembers" what the BBS has said to it. If you want to take another look at something that went across the screen a few minutes ago, just move the text "down" with the FCTN X key, the ↓. Your computer can only "look back" about six screen-fulls of text. You should move the text back to where it belongs before typing anything on the screen, or else the display will become very confusing. Of course, you do this with the FCTN E, the ↑. To move a whole page at a time, press CTRL 7 and then FCTN X or FCTN E.

If the BBS starts doing something that takes very long, or that you're not interested in, you can sometimes interrupt it with CTRL / (press the "slash" key while holding down CTRL), or with CTRL X, or CTRL . ("period" with CTRL), or CTRL C.

If you have a speech synthesizer, pressing CTRL 1 will cause the TI to speak all the text shown on the TV screen.

Finally, when you end your session and AFTER you hang up the phone, press CTRL 0 ("zero" with CTRL), to exit the terminal emulator.

Keeping A Record

It is possible, while receiving information from another computer or

BBS, to make a permanent record of what you are viewing on the screen. This is a very worthwhile feature of TERMINAL EMULATOR II, as it allows you to save a lot of information while you are connected to a computer located a great distance away and most likely costing you a long distance phone call. You can save information quickly, without having to write it down by hand. Once saved, you can hang up the phone and have a leisurely look at what you've recorded.

To make a permanent record of what is on your screen, press CTRL 2 (OUTPUT). The screen will immediately change to a display that asks the name of the device to which you wish to save the information on the screen. You have several choices. You may choose a disk drive (DSK1), or a cassette recorder (CS1), or the TI thermal printer (TP). You may choose any device capable of saving or printing information, which you have connected to your computer.

Go ahead and enter the name of an appropriate device to save the screen to. Notice we keep saying "save the screen". The computer's memory contains more information than is actually visible on the screen, as you may have already discovered by using the FCTN E (↑) or FCTN X (↓) keys. However, only what is visible on the screen at the time you press CTRL 2 will be saved on your printer or disk drive.

When the screen information has been saved for you, the screen will return to display the information from the other computer, unchanged.

If you saved the screen to a disk drive file each time you press the CTRL 2 (OUTPUT) keys, you will get a message that asks if you want to save the screen to the same device. If you answer "YES", the new information will be added to the end of what you previously saved. If you answer "NO", the file will be closed and you no longer can save information into that file, but must create a new file name. At the end of your terminal session, you must safely close your disk file by pressing CTRL 0 to EXIT the terminal emulator.

If you save information to a printer such as the EPSON MX-80, you may want to print it with 80 characters on a line. Since your TV screen is only 36 or 40 characters wide, the computer normally "wraps" long lines. This means it splits them into two or more short lines that will fit on the screen. Many printers can handle a longer line, so you may turn off the WRAP feature by pressing CTRL 5 (WRAP). Pressing CTRL 5 a second time will turn WRAP back on. You do not have to turn off the wrap feature. If you leave it on, the printout will look just like your TV screen. *WARNING: Pressing CTRL 5 erases the screen memory! If you want to print 80-column lines, you must turn off the WRAP* **before** *receiving the information from the other computer or BBS.*

Uploading and Downloading

The last feature we are going to mention here is the File Transfer function. File transfer lets you send or receive whole files of information instead of just one screen full. TEXNET allows you use this feature to copy programs and games from its software library, and to contribute some of your own programs or games for others to use. You can only use this feature between two TI 99/4A computers or with a BBS that supports this special function of the TI. Check with the BBS you are calling if you are not sure whether it supports this feature.

If you have a file on your cassette recorder you wish to send to another TI computer or BBS, here is how it's done:

After you have called the other TI computer and everything is working normally, press CTRL 4 (TRANS). The computer will now ask you to give the name of the device you are sending the file from. You will type "CS1" (CS2 is not allowed). Because cassette files have no individual names, file transfer will begin immediately. There are some rules for file transfers between cassette recorders and cassette recorders and disk drives. You should read the Terminal Emulator Handbook before attempting these types of tranfers.

If your files or programs are on disk and you wish to send them to another disk, the process is the same. After you type "DSK1" you will be asked to give the name of the file you wish to transfer.

What about being on the receiving end of things? It's easy! When another computer transfers a file to you, a message appears on your screen that says "HOST HAS STARTED FILE TRANSFER". If you don't want to receive, simply press CTRL 3 (CANCEL). However, your curiosity should get the best of you. Just wait a bit and the second message will appear: "PLEASE ENTER DEVICE NAME TO OUTPUT DATA TO". If you answer "CS1" the transfer will begin. If you answer "DSK1", then you will be asked to give a file name the computer can open and put the data into. When the transfer is complete the computer will go back to whatever was happening before the transfer began.

Special Characters

For the benefit of programmers familiar with ASCII code, most of the ASCII characters can be generated by the Terminal Emulator. These tables give the correspondences:

Press	*Comments*
CTRL A	Start of heading
CTRL B	Start of text
CTRL C	End of text
CTRL D	End of tranmission
CTRL E	Enquiry
CTRL F	Acknowledge
CTRL G	Bell
CTRL H	Backspace
CTRL I	Horizontal tabulation
CTRL J	Line feed
CTRL K	Vertical tabulation
CTRL L	Form feed
ENTER	Carriage return
CTRL N	Shift out
CTRL O	Shift in
CTRL P	Data link escape
CTRL Q	Device control 1 (X-ON)
CTRL R	Device control 2
CTRL S	Device control 3 (X-OFF)
CTRL T	Device control 4
CTRL U	Negative acknowledge
CTRL V	Synchronous idle
CTRL W	End of transmission block

Press	*Comments*
CTRL X	Cancel
CTRL Y	End of medium
CTRL Z	Substitute
CTRL .	Escape
CTRL ;	File separator
CTRL =	Group separator
CTRL 8	Record separator
CTRL 9	Unit separator
FCTN V	Delete
CTRL /	BREAK
FCTN Z	\ (backslash)
FCTN W	~ (tilde)
FCTN A	| (vertical line)
FCTN C	` (file separator)
FCTN R	[(open bracket)
FCTN T	] (close bracket)
FCTN F	{ (open brace)
FCTN G	} (close brace)
FCTN U	_ (underline)
SHIFT /	- (dash)
FCTN I	? (question mark)
FCTN O	' (apostrophe)
FCTN P	" (quotation mark)

YOUR FRIENDLY BBS
BBS

YOUR FRIENDLY BBS

There are more than 500 Bulletin Board Services located throughout the country that you can contact using the information provided in this book.

Even though many of these BBS's are designed to operate with other computers (Apple, Atari, PET, TRS-80, etc.), you can get on-line with them to leave a message, chat with the System Operator (SYSOP) or review the latest computer news and events. But, don't forget: you can download software from TEXNET and will soon be able to contact the worlds' first privately owned 99/4A bulletin board, T.I.B.B.S. (See page 117.)

We'll also introduce you to some FREE and interesting recreational services that are waiting for your call.

To help you explore this fascinating world, we've included a directory of these Bulletin Boards. Call them up and take advantage of the services they have to offer...it will expand your horizons. You might discover that some of these BBS's have special TI information sections...we did!

You've Made Contact!

You've just made your first contact with a BBS. Your heart beats faster, your fingers poise over your computer's keyboard ready to respond to any question that might appear on the screen. You want to call in friends and family to show them this marvel of communications, but a cold sweat breaks out on your forehead as the question, "How many nulls?" scrolls onto your screen. "What do I do now?" you ask. "What's the right answer? What's a 'null' anyhow?"

To make your first contact with a BBS exciting instead of traumatic, we'll help you through your first BBS experience.

DIFFERENT BULLETIN BOARDS HAVE LOTS IN COMMON

First, you should know that most BBS's ask the same kinds of questions at sign-on and accept the same types of commands when you're past the sign-on stage. This makes it easy for you to call up and "talk" to virtually any type of BBS.

We'll show you how to sign-on to a typical BBS, share a few helpful hints, then list the commands of some of the more common BBS's and explain each command's function. Then you can make your first contact with confidence!

SIGNING ON

After you "dial" a BBS, you will hear a few rings followed by a steady tone. You've got 'em! If you are using an acoustic modem, plug your headset into the two rubber cups. If you have a direct-connect modem, communications will begin automatically, or at the flip of a switch.

HELPFUL HINT 1

If your screen remains blank after you think that contact has been made, press ENTER a few times...that usually gets the BBS's attention!

Now that you've got the BBS's attention it will start bossing you around. The first thing that most BBS's will tell you to do is: PRESS ENTER (or "RETURN"). After you've done that, the BBS will start bragging about itself. The Itsy Bitsy Bulletin Board Service (IBBS) of San Jose, California, begins each transmission by drawing a picture of a rocket ship followed by a short introductory message that tells you how great it is! Have patience, the BBS operators (SYSOPS) are providing you with a great FREE service and get a kick out of showing off a little.

HELPFUL HINT 2

Some BBS's might ask the intimidating question: "How many nulls?". The answer is simple: "0".

You might also be asked: "Do you need line feeds?" Just answer "YES".

When asked what your screen size is, answer back with a resounding "80". (No, it's not, but your computer can take care of itself! If you say 80, then transcriptions to a printer will be "full width" instead of only filling half the width of the paper. (See p. 106 –107.)

If you are asked "Can you receive lower case letters?", answer, "YES".

WHAT'S YOUR NAME?

If you know your name, this part is really easy! After you press ENTER, most BBS's will ask for your name, then the City and State you are calling from. Answer these questions and your screen will say something like: "WAIT A MINUTE, I'M LOGGING YOU TO MY FILES." So, wait a minute!

WHAT'S THIS "PASSWORD" STUFF?

Some BBS's seem downright impertinent. Instead of asking for your name, they'll ask you for a Password! Don't Panic!! The reason some Bulletin Boards want their users to have Passwords is so they can keep out the "rif-raf". Since you're not rif-raf *you qualify for a Password.* Getting one is usually very simple and straightforward.

You'll be asked to enter up to seven or eight characters. My Password is my birthdate...41793. (April 17, 1893). Every time you call this BBS, use your Password to move into its system. If you use a different Password for each BBS that requires one, things could become a bit confusing, so don't forget to write it down next to the BBS's phone number. It's like remembering your Secret Code for your friendly ATM (Automated Teller Machine) at the bank. *Use something simple.*

YOU'RE NOW INSIDE THE BBS!

You've made it! You've seen the BBS's grand opening show, "logged-in", and are ready to start using all the FREE services this BBS has to offer.

You will now be asked something like: "IS THIS YOUR FIRST TIME HERE?". *Answer "YES" and you'll be given complete instructions.* To *S*top these instructions as they whiz by on your screen, you usually press the CTRL (CONTROL) key plus the "S" key. To allow the message to continue to scroll, just press CTRL (CONTROL) plus the "Q" key.

ALPHABET SOUP

If you are a smarty and answered "NO", this is what you might see: COMMAND (A,B,C,D,E,F,G,H,K,L,O,Q,R,S,T,U,W,X,Z):

Looks like alphabet soup! Actually, these letters represent the keys you press to communicate with the BBS.

For example, if you press the letter "F", you will be shown the complete file of programs that can be downloaded. If you press the letter "R" you'll be able to retrieve messages from the bulletin board.

Remember, most systems are very similar. Almost all of these letter abbreviations will work on any system. Just to play it safe, answer "YES", when the Bulletin Board asks if this is your first visit and review the instructions.

The goin' is easy once you're in contact with a BBS. If you're ever in trouble, just type "?" or "H" to review the operating instructions. . . if that doesn't help type "C" and chat with the System Operator. Notice that many BBS's have lists of other BBS telephone numbers. This is your key to a vast number of other Bulletin Boards and FREE resources.

Here's what pressing each of these letters will do on a typical BBS:

Typical BBS Instructions

(Adapted from an ATARI BBS run by GRAFex Co., in California)

B—Reprints System Operator's bulletins to users.

C—Lists the name and address of prior callers to the system.

D—Download program. Downloads programs on this system to your terminal. (Until Ralph Fowler introduces his terminal software you won't be able to take advantage of this valuable option. See *World's First Privately Owned 99/4A Bulletin Board,* Page 117).

E—Enter a message to the system. After inputting "E", the next steps are self explanatory.

F—Lists programs and files available for download. Choose the Section # of the type of file you want to download. We are currently offering: BASIC, and MICROSOFT BASIC programs. We also have TEXT FILES, DOCUMENTATION (for this BBS, as well as for some of the programs on the system), AMATEUR RADIO.

G—Goodbye. This is the command used to exit the system.

H—Help. Prints this list.

K—Kill a message. Deletes your message from the system.

L—Toggles linefeed after carriage return (on/off).

O—Lists other BBS's you might want to contact.

Q—Quick scan. Scans message titles only.

R—Retrieve a message or messages from system. You may retrieve more than one message at a time by separating message numbers with a comma, or a group of messages by separating with a hyphen (-).

S—Scan messages. Scans message titles; shows you who the message is to and who it's from. You may scan more than one message at a time by separating message numbers with a comma. A *group* of messages should be separated with a hyphen (-).

T—Shows you the current time (PST), day of week and date.

U—Upload your program to system. Uploaded programs are put into a special section until they can be checked. (Not currently available to TI Home Computer owners.)

W—Repeats welcome message sent when user first logs on system.

X—Shifts to and from the Expert User Mode. After pressing "X" you qualify as an Expert User, and will *not be shown* the menus at each input prompt.

Z—Leave a message to the System Operator. Your message will be printed on our printer.

OTHER COMMANDS YOU MIGHT ENCOUNTER ON OTHER SYSTEMS

?—the question mark is often used to ask for help in place of the "H" command.

C—is very often used to allow you to "Chat" with the System Operator.

I—when you type "I" on some systems, a description of the programs they have on file will be listed.

BYE or OFF—"G" to say "goodbye".

Q—is also sometimes used to say "goodbye".

Dive in, get on-line today and start communicating!

T.I.B.B.S.
THE WORLD'S FIRST PRIVATELY OWNED 99/4A BULLETIN BOARD
(404) 425-5254

In May, 1983, a major telecommunications milestone was passed and congratulations poured in from enthusiastic TI home computer owners. Ralph Fowler of Kennesaw, Georgia had made a major contribution to TI owners everywhere—he developed a software package that turns the TI-99/4A into a BBS base station!

Other personal computers (Apple, Atari, Commodore, IBM PC and TRS-80) have firmly established a network of privately-run bulletin boards that allow their users to get the latest computer news, exchange ideas and messages, and up- and download public domain software. Now, with the introduction of T.I.B.B.S. TI home computer owners will soon be able to do the same.

T.I.B.B.S. currently offers a complete electronic message bulletin board and information service. You can read and leave messages, save, edit, and chat with the System Operator (SYSOP).

After Ralph irons the bugs out of this Phase I system he'll add up- and downloading capabilities to his software. Then he plans to introduce terminal software for the home computer user.

WHY DID RALPH DO IT?

"I've always been a supporter of TI. All home computers are good but the TI caught me. I got interested in BBS's at work, after using a terminal, and always wanted to have one of my own."

Ralph's challenge wasn't easy. He said that, "I've been working on T.I.B.B.S. for six months." His final product was well worth the effort.

Ralph is an Energy Coordinator at a local school district, and did all the T.I.B.B.S. development in the evenings and during long weekends.

WHAT YOU NEED TO START YOUR OWN TI-99/4A BBS

Ralph gave us this shopping list when we asked what we'd need to start our own base station:

- TI-99/4A computer
- 48K Memory
- Direct Connect Auto-answer Modem
- Expansion Box
- RS-232 Card
- Double-sided disk drive or two single-sided disk drives. (System will work with one disk drive but the message file bank will be limited.)
- Disk Controller
- Extended BASIC
- T.I.B.B.S. Software and cable

T.I.B.B.S. SOFTWARE

Ralph plans to sell the T.I.B.B.S. software (complete with instructions) for "around $50.00". Ralph said that, "this will just about cover my development costs, cost of packaging, and shipping." Ralph added, "I'll support my software and work with people who want to start their own TI BBS's."

WANT TO BE A PIONEER?

If you'd like to be a TI Users' pioneer and start your own BBS, or just talk via modem to T.I.B.B.S. in Kennesaw, Georgia, you can contact Ralph Fowler by writing to him c/o:

> Lobo Inc.
> P.O. Box 383
> Kennesaw, GA 30144
> BBS#: (404) 425-5254

To give you a feeling for Ralph's exciting new service, we called T.I.B.B.S. and transcribed our conversation. (We learned later that Message #7 was from Anda, a blind girl from Florida. Ralph told us that she used an optical/touch system to communicate with his BBS.)

In Contact with The World's First TI 99/4A BBS

Following is a transcript of a call I made to T.I.B.B.S.—the world's first TI 99/4A home computer BBS. My responses are in boldface type:

THANK YOU FOR CALLING

T.I.B.B.S. ATLANTA

RALPH FOWLER
SYSTEM OPERATOR (SYSOP)

PLEASE LOG IN
NAME: **DAVID HELLER**
CITY, STATE: **CUPERTINO, CA**
DAVID HELLER IN CUPERTINO, CA
CORRECT: (Y/N) **Y**
CHECKING USERLOG... STANDBY
YOU ARE A NEW USER. PLEASE ENTER A PASSWORD OF UP TO 5 CHARACTERS. A PASSWORD IS NOT REQUIRED, BUT IT WILL HELP SAFEGUARD YOUR MESSAGES.

PASSWORD? **ABCD**
PASSWORD IS ABCD
CORRECT? **Y**
LOGGING DAVID HELLER TO DISK

BULLETINS:

THIS IS A BULLETIN BOARD SYSTEM FOR THE TEXAS INSTRUMENTS TI 99/4A HOME COMPUTER.

THIS BASE STATION SOFTWARE CAN RUN ON A 48K TI 99/4A WITH EXTENDED BASIC, A DIRECT CONNECT HAYES SMARTMODEM AND AT LEAST ONE SINGLE SIDED DISK DRIVE.

YOU ARE PARTICIPATING IN A FIELD TEST OF THE PROGRAM, AND YOU MAY ENCOUNTER A FEW ERRORS. IF YOU DO, PLEASE TRY AND REMEMBER WHAT YOU WERE DOING WHEN THE ERROR OCCURRED.

IF YOU HAVE ANY SUGGESTIONS OR COMMENTS, PLEASE LEAVE THEM IN A MESSAGE ADDRESSED TO: "SYSOP"

YOU ARE CALLER # 58
THERE ARE 29 MESSAGES ON FILE
RANGING FROM # 1 to # 29
CHAT IS TURNED ON
COMMAND (? = HELP) **?**

MENU:

(R)ead messages (E)nter message
(S)can messages (C)hat with sysop
(G)oodbye (M)essage count
(O)ther systems
COMMAND (? = HELP) **R**

READ WHICH MESSAGE? (1 - 29) **28**

MESSAGE # 28
TO SYSOP
FROM TOM BOISSEAU
RE: T.I.B.B.S.
DATE 7/01/83

I CAN NOT TELL YOU HOW GLAD I AM THAT SOMEONE FINALLY WENT TO ALL THE WORK AND CAME UP WITH A BBS FOR THE TI 99/4A. YOU ARE TO BE CONGRATULATED ON ALL YOUR EFFORTS. I HAD THOUGHT OF TRYING TO DO THE SAME MYSELF, BUT AFTER HEARING ALL THAT YOU HAVE GONE THROUGH I DOUBT THAT I WOULD HAVE SUCCEEDED IN COMPLETING THE PROJECT. AGAIN, CONGRATULATIONS.

END OF MESSAGE 28

COMMAND (? = HELP) **R**
READ WHICH MESSAGE? (1 - 29) **7**

MESSAGE # 7
TO SYSOP
FROM ANDA
RE: T.I.B.B.S.
DATE 7/01/83

REALLY SUPER! RALPH. I AM DELIGHTED TO HAVE YOU SHARE THIS NEW BBS FOR THE TI 99/4A WITH ME.

GOOD LUCK! IF I CAN EVER BE OF HELP FEEL FREE TO CALL ME.....
SERIALLY YOURS! ANDA

COMMAND (? = HELP) **E**

DO YOU WANT SOME HELPFUL INFORMATION ABOUT HOW TO ENTER MESSAGES?
(Y/N) **Y**

MESSAGE HELP (UPDATED 7/4/83)

MESSAGES MAY BE ENTERED IN BOTH UPPER AND LOWER CASE.

REMEMBER THAT YOU ARE ONLY ALLOWED 12 LINES OF 40 CHARACTERS EACH

A ROW OF 40 "UNDERLINE" CHARACTERS WILL BE PRINTED TO SHOW YOU WHEN YOU ARE APPROACHING THE END OF THE INPUT LINE.

IF YOU ENTER MORE THAN 40 CHARACTERS ON A LINE, THE LINE WILL AUTOMATICALLY BE SHORTENED TO 40 CHARACTERS. IF THIS HAPPENS, THE SHORTENED LINE WILL BE PRINTED BACK TO YOU FOR YOUR APPROVAL.

DO NOT USE THE CONTROL H/BACKSPACE KEY TO ERASE MISTAKES. USE "FCTN V" INSTEAD. AS YOU RUB OUT A CHARACTER, THAT CHARACTER WILL BE ECHOED BACK TO YOU.

IF YOU PRESS CONTROL R DURING ANY INPUT, I WILL PRINT MY INPUT BUFFER BACK TO YOU. THIS IS A GREAT HELP WHEN EDITING A LINE.

END OF MESSAGE HELP
THIS WILL BE MESSAGE # 30
WHO IS MESSAGE TO? **SYSOP**
FROM **DAVID HELLER**
DATE= 07/08/83
SUBJECT? **MY ADDRESS**
ENTER TEXT BELOW
12 LINES MAXIMUM
40 CHARS. MAX PER LINE
ENTER A NULL LINE TO QUIT
LINE 1

C/O ENRICH/OHAUS
LINE 2

2325 PARAGON DRIVE
LINE 3

SAN JOSE, CA 95131
LINE 4

OPTION?
(S)ave (L)ist (R)edo line
(A)bort (C)ontinue **S**
SAVING MSG. NO. 30
UPDATING SUMMARY FILE
UPDATING MESSAGE FILE

COMMAND (? = HELP) **R**

READ WHICH MESSAGE? (1 - 29) **4**

MESSAGE # 4
TO ANDA
FROM RALPH FOWLER
RE: HELLO
DATE 5/22/83
HI THERE. I'VE HEARD A LOT ABOUT YOU OVER THE PAST FEW WEEKS. I HOPE THAT YOU ENJOY THIS PROTOTYPE OF THE TIBBS SYSTEM. SEE YOU LATER. RALPH FOWER

END OF MESSAGE 4

COMMAND (? = HELP) **R**

READ WHICH MESSAGE? (1 - 29) **18**
MESSAGE # 18
TO RALPH
FROM Marshall Gordon
RE: Congratulations
DATE 7/01/83
It really is a professional job. It's as good as most BBS's in the Atlanta

area. It's really good to know that the TI finally has its own privately run BBS system.

Congratulations on the great job you've done.

Marshall Gordon
ATLANTA 99/4A USERS GROUP

END OF MESSAGE 18

COMMAND (? = HELP) **G**

GOODBYE.

TEXNET

TEXNET Information Service (a service of Source Telecomputing Corporation) is **not** a free resource, but it is certainly a valuable one for all TI home computer owners.

The following is excerpted from Texas Instruments' April 1983 *Home Computer Newsletter:*

By subscribing to the TEXNET Information Service, users can turn their Home Computers into information centers. TEXNET brings 99/4A users the services of The SOURCE, a computer software service for business, education, and home entertainment, plus access to TI news and information.

Among the special services available to TEXNET subscribers are the following:

TI NEWS—An electronic newsletter with product and technical announcements from Texas Instruments.

TI SOFTWARE EXCHANGE—Software exchange service (with) hundreds of free programs you can review and save with your Home Computer.

TI VOICE CHAT—Spoken, interactive communication from other on-line users made possible by using the optional speech synthesizer.

TI PHONETIC DICTIONARY—A growing library of over 2,000 entries; offers phonetic spelling of words that are helpful when programming with the "text-to-speech" feature of the Terminal Emulator II.

TI HELP—How to use TEXNET

TI SOFTWARE DIRECTORY—A catalog of software that can be purchased through TI dealers.

TI USERS' GROUPS—A nationwide listing of Texas Instruments Users' Groups and who to contact.

TI SERVICE CENTERS—Listing of locations for maintenance and repairs on Texas Instruments equipment.

TI GRAPHIC LIBRARY—An expanding graphics library that users can view or download for personal use.

TI MUSIC AND SOUND LIBRARY—A library of musical scores and sounds available for use in your own programs.

THE SOURCE—Over 1000 information and communication services.

Equipment you'll need:

To access TEXNET you'll need: a TI-99/4 or TI-99/4A computer, Terminal Emulator II Cartridge, an RS-232 Interface Card (plugs into a Peripheral Expansion System), and a 300 baud Phone Modem. A printer is optional. And, of course, you'll need a subscription to TEXNET!

How to tap TEXNET

To tap TEXNET you simply dial a local number available in more than 400 cities. Once you're in touch, you'll be asked for your private

ID account number. Once this is entered, you simply enter commands using plain English.

Additional Services

Subscribers can also receive: up-to-the minute national and international news, financial and business information, market reports, and international document research.

Travel services such as checking late flight schedules, making airline, hotel, and auto reservations, plus gathering information about restaurants and lodging places is all a snap with TEXNET.

How much does all this cost?

There is an initial subscription fee of $100 plus usage rates.

I'd like more information!

If you want more information about TEXNET call toll-free: 1-800-336-3330. (In some states the prefix "1" is not required.)

TEXNET User's Manual

The TEXNET User's Manual provides step-by-step instructions to help you get the most from this valuable service. We kept it at our side when we called TEXNET.

The TEXNET Software Exchange

Since this book is primarily about free software, we decided to see what was available on TEXNET's Software Exchange.

The Software Exchange is a constantly changing library of software which includes games, graphics, educational, business and professional programs all available *free* to TEXNET users. The programs are gathered and managed by the International 99/4 Home Computer Users' Group, and can be downloaded to your TI Home Computer equipped with a Disk Memory System and Terminal Emulator II

Command Module.

If you've developed a program that you'd like to place on the exchange you can do this via modem, or by sending it to the International 99/4 Home Computer Users' Group. (See Mini Profile, Page 58.)

A WEALTH OF FREE PUBLIC DOMAIN SOFTWARE

We contacted TEXNET and downloaded the following software list to give you an idea of the wealth of *free* programs available to subscribers:

Table Of Contents
Basic And Extended Basic Programs

NEW GAMES

BOMBS AWAY
DARTS
INSANITY (XBASIC)
SPACE PILOTS (XBASIC)
TANK COMMAND (XBASIC)
ADVENTURE
BASE ALERT (XBASIC)
BATTLEGROUND (XBASIC)
INVASION WAVE (XBASIC)

GAMES

CARS AND CARCASSES
CRAPS
NIMBLE
AIRCOMBAT
BATTLESHIP
GO-HOME
LEXICALITY
PUZZLE-15
WHITE HOLES
ZAP A BALL
GOLF
TIC-TAC-TOE (WITH LIGHT PEN)
TOURING
STARS
LIFT
CAMEL
WORD GAME
CHECKERS
DOCKING
ARTILLERY
DRAGON MAZE
LAST ROBOT
LUNAR LANDER
OBSTACLE COURSE
MASTERMIND
SCHMOO

CRAZY LINES
BATTLERS
MINER
ONE-OR-TWO
SCRAMBLE
SUPERMAN
OTHELLO
YAHTZEE
ALIEN
BATTLE OF IAPETUS
INBETWEEN
SQUARES
KING
LINE UP
MAZE
SCORCHER
SPLAT
FOUR IN A ROW
DODGEM
MOTOCROSS
NOMAD
PSCHOLOGY
SPACE SCOUT
SPACE INVADERS
STELLAR EXPLORER
STOCK MARKET
CHICKEN HELPER (XBASIC)
HOT-DOG (XBASIC)
WARFISH (XBASIC)
WOODS-WALK
AIR CONTROLLER (XBASIC)
LARGO DOWNS (XBASIC)
ZAN QUEST (XBASIC)
STARDOGER (XBASIC)
EX-GOLF (XBASIC)
MATCH-UP

MUSIC

GODFATHER
BEWITCHED
INVENTION IN B (BACH)
MUSIC BOX DANCER
NEVER ON SUNDAY
STAR TREK THEME
MUSICAL TRANSPOSITION
SNOOPY CHRISTMAS

EDUCATION

ARITHMAGRAPHS
COLOR CRAYON
CAPITOLS
CAREERS
FRACTIONS
PRESIDENTS
SPELL
SPELLDOWN
SPELLING
FLAG-O-RAMA
TENSE
COLOR MATH
SPELL AND SCORE
TIME AND SPEED
WORD-TWINS (TE-II)

BUSINESS & FINANCIAL

FINANCIAL MATH
ADDRESSES
P.E.R.T.
C.P.M.
HANDICAPPER
MAILLIST
CREDIT CARD
GENEOLOGY
KITCHENS AIDS I
LISTS

UTILITY & MISCELLANEOUS

AUTO-LOGON
HAUNTED HOUSE
SEAHORSE
STARS
LOVE
VISIONS
LOWER-CASE
MAZE-MAKER
SAFETY AWARENESS
VGL-LETTERS
TERMINAL DATA RETRIEVAL
DATA RETRIEVE WITH
(LOWER CASE)

Downloading is a snap

The downloading procedure is simple and straightforward. Each program has an identifying number, and you simply enter the number of your chosen program when asked if you want to download. You are given a short description of the program before it is sent, and then given the option of accepting it or going on to another. Here is the actual conversation we had with TEXNET when we asked to download the game "EX-GOLF". Our responses are in boldface type:

TI-XCHNG **P0065**

NAME: EX-GOLF

DESCRIPTION:
TRY YOUR LUCK ON THE TI COUNTRY
CLUB COURSE. SET YOUR SWING
STRENGTHS AND WATCH YOUR GOLF
BALL FLY.

SOFTWARE REQUIRED:
EXTENDED BASIC

HARDWARE REQUIRED:
JOYSTICKS

DISK SIZE: 35 SECTORS.

SPECIAL INSTRUCTIONS: NONE.

DO YOU WISH TO DOWNLOAD THIS PROGRAM? **Y**
STARTING DOWNLOAD....

TI LOGO is available on TEXNET

The LOGO section of TEXNET should be of special interest to parents and educators. Here's what was available for downloading when we called.

TI LOGO PROCEDURE EXCHANGE

THIS DATABASE CONTAINS PROCEDURES WRITTEN FOR TI LOGO, WHICH CAN BE DOWNLOADED OR TRANSFERRED TO A TI HOME COMPUTER WITH A DISK MEMORY SYSTEM AND TERMINAL EMULATOR II COMMAND MODULE.

ALL PROCEDURES HAVE BEEN CHECKED FOR OPERATIONAL ABILITIES. SOME PROCEDURES LACK OPERATING INSTRUCTIONS AND OTHERS MAY CONTAIN

SLIGHT BUGS, BUT THESE DON'T IMPAIR GENERAL USAGE.

USERS ARE ENCOURAGED TO SUBMIT IMPROVEMENTS TO THESE PROCEDURES AS WELL AS PROCEDURES OF THEIR OWN BY CONTACTING TI9999.

Index

PROCEDURES

PROCEDURES WITH SHAPES AND TILES

Downloading a Frog!

PROCEDURE NAME:**FROG**

PROCEDURE DESCIPTION: CREATES A FROG IN A POND AND HAS GOOD ANIMATION.

SOFTWARE REQUIRED: TI LOGO.

HARDWARE REQUIRED: MEMORY EXPANSION AND DISK OR CASSETTE.

DISK SIZE: 21 SECTORS.

Summing It Up

TEXNET is a service loaded with valuable resources. But, it is not free. If you'd like information mailed to you send your request to:

TEXNET Information Service
Source Telecomputing Corporation
1616 Anderson Road
McLean, Virginia 22102

DIRECTORY OF TI BULLETIN BOARDS[1]

*—24 hour operation

T.I.B.B.S.

CA	T.I.B.B.S.	404-425-5254
DC	WASHINGTON	301-681-5065

LIVING TREE

CA	LVNG VIDEOTEXT	415-327-8876 *#
CA	FAR WEST LABS	415-565-3037 *
CA	COMPUTER PLUS	408-735-8181 *

DIAL-YOUR-MATCH

CA	DIAL-YOUR-MATCH #26	209-298-1328 *
CA	DIAL-YOUR-MATCH #1	213-842-3322 *
CA	DIAL-YOUR-MATCH #11	213-242-1882 *
CA	DIAL-YOUR-MATCH #4	213-783-2305 *
CA	DIAL-YOUR-MATCH #9	213-345-1047 *
CA	DIAL-YOUR-MATCH #22	213-990-6830 *
CA	DIAL-YOUR-MATCH #17	415-991-4911 *
GA	DIAL-YOUR-MATCH #3	912-233-0863 *
MA	DIAL-YOUR-MATCH #18	617-334-6369 *
NC	DIAL-YOUR-MATCH #20	919-362-0676 *
NE	DIAL-YOUR-MATCH #23	402-571-8942 *
NJ	DIAL-YOUR-MATCH #14	201-272-3686 *
TX	DIAL-YOUR-MATCH #24	713-783-4136 *
TX	DIAL-YOUR-MATCH #12	713-556-1531 *
WA	DIAL-YOUR-MATCH #16	206-256-6624 *

---

[1]Every effort was made to insure that the information provided in this directory is current and accurate. Because Bulletin Boards may change their phone numbers, we cannot accept responsibility or be held liable for any errors.

PUBLIC ACCESS MESSAGE SYSTEMS

We have included this valuable list of Public Access Message Systems to allow you to explore the many types of BBS's and services available to you.

This directory was downloaded from the People's Message System, of Santee, California. Call this, and other Bulletin Boards, to get their latest list of active Bulletin Boards and services.

* *

PUBLIC ACCESS MESSAGE (and file transfer) SYSTEMS

Compliments of Peoples' Message System, Santee CA
(619) 561-7277
Compiled and maintained by Bill Blue
(with a lot of help from his friends)

Please send updates/corrections to:
PMS Santee, TCB117, 70315,1305 or BBLUE
* *

*24 denotes 24-hour operation
#1 denotes original system of that type
-rb denotes call, let ring once and call back
-rl religious orientation
! new system or new number to existing system
$ Supports VADIC 1200 baud operation
& Supports 212A 1200 baud operation
% Supports BAUDOT operation

Regular updates of this list may be found on
CompuServe MAUG XA4, The Source PUBLIC 112,
and most participating independent PMS systems.
Current filesize is 36,252 bytes.

ABBS ABACUS II, Toledo, OH..................(419) 865 1594
ABBS AGS, Atlanta, GA.......................(404) 733 3461*24
ABBS Akron Digital Group, Akron, OH..........(216) 745 7855*24
ABBS Apple Crate I, Seattle, WA..............(206) 935 9119
ABBS Apple Crate II, Seattle, WA.............(206) 244 5438
ABBS Apple-Med, Iowa City, IA................(319) 353 6528
ABBS Apple-Mate, New York, NY................(201) 864 5345
ABBS Baileys Computer Store, Augusta, GA.....(404) 790 8614
ABBS Baton Rouge, LA.........................(504) 291 1360
ABBS Byte Shop, Ft. Lauderdale, FL...........(305) 486 2983
ABBS Byte Shop, Miami, FL....................(305) 261 3639
ABBS Calvary Mission Church, Mnpls, MN.......(612) 471 0252-rl
ABBS CCNJ, Pompton Plains, NJ................(201) 835 7228
ABBS Century Next Computers, St. Louis, MO...(314) 442 6502
ABBS Charlotte, NC...........................(704) 364 5254
ABBS CODE, Glen Ellyn IL.....................(312) 537 7063*24
ABBS Colortron Computer, WI..................(414) 637 9990*24
ABBS Compumart, Ottawa, Ontario, Canada......(613) 725 2243
ABBS Computerland, Fremont, CA...............(415) 794 9314
ABBS Computer Corner, Amarillo, TX...........(806) 355 5610
ABBS Computer Conspiracy, Santa Monica, CA...(213) 829 1140
ABBS Computer Crossroads, Columbia, MD.......(301) 730 0922
ABBS Computer Lab, Memphis, TN...............(901) 761 4743
ABBS Computer Room, Kalamazoo, MI............(616) 382 0101
ABBS Computer Store, Toledo, OH..............(419) 531 3845
ABBS Dallas Info Board.......................(214) 248 4539
ABBS Denver, CO..............................(303) 759 2625
ABBS Detroit, MI.............................(313) 477 4471
ABBS Electro-Mart, Spokane, WA...............(509) 534 2419*24
ABBS Fort Walton Beach, Destin, FL...........(904) 243 1257
ABBS Gamemaster, Chicago, IL.................(312) 475 4884*24
ABBS Hayward, CA.............................(415) 881 5662
ABBS Illini Microcomputer, Naperville, IL....(312) 420 7995
ABBS Ketchikan, AK...........................(907) 225 6789
ABBS Livingston, NJ..........................(201) 994 9620*24
ABBS Madam Bokeatha Society, Houston, TX.....(713) 455 9502
ABBS Michigan Apple-Fone, Southfield, MI.....(313) 357 1422
ABBS Newport Beach, CA.......................(714) 645 5256*24
ABBS Omaha, NE...............................(402) 339 7809
ABBS PCnet, San Francisco, CA................(415) 863 4703*24
ABBS Pacific Palasades, Los Angeles, CA......(213) 459 6400
ABBS Peoria, IL..............................(309) 692 6502

ABBS Phoenix, AZ..............................(602) 898 0891
ABBS Pirates Cove, Long Island, NY...........(516) 698 4008
ABBS Rogers Park, Chicago, IL.................(312) 973 2227
ABBS Software Sorcery, Herndon, VA...........(703) 471 0610
ABBS South of Market, San Francisco, CA......(415) 469 8111
ABBS St. Louis, MO...........................(314) 838 7784*24
ABBS Teledunjon I, Dallas, TX................(817) 469 1626
ABBS Teledunjon II, Dallas, TX...............(214) 530 0858
ABBS Teledunjon III, Dallas, TX..............(214) 960 7654
ABBS The Moon, Dallas, TX....................(214) 931 3437*24
ABBS Turnersville, NJ........................(609) 228 1149
ABBS Vancouver, B.C..........................(604) 437 7001
ABBS Vermont, Essex Junction, VT.............(802) 879 4981*24
ABBS West Palm Beach, FL.....................(305) 848 3802
ABBS Rob Roy Computer, Yakima, WA............(509) 575 7704
ABBS Youngs Elect Svc., College Station, TX..(713) 693 3462*24
ABBS #X, Atlanta, GA.........................(404) 256 1549

A-C-C-E-S-S Annapolis, MD....................(301) 267 7666*24
A-C-C-E-S-S Olympia, WA......................(206) 866 9043*24
A-C-C-E-S-S Phoenix, AZ..................#1 (602) 996 9709*24
A-C-C-E-S-S Phoenix, AZ....................&(602) 957 4428*24
A-C-C-E-S-S Phoenix, AZ.....................(602) 274 5964
A-C-C-E-S-S Scotsdale, AZ...................(602) 998 9411*24
A-C-C-E-S-S Wyckoff, NJ.....................(201) 891 7441*24

BBS IBM Hostcomm Atlanta, GA................!(404) 252 4146
BBS IBM Hostcomm Claremont, CA..............!(714) 624 1767
BBS IBM Hostcomm Fairfax, VA................!(703) 978 9592*24
BBS IBM Hostcomm Fairfax, VA................!(703) 978 0921*24
BBS IBM Hostcomm Fairfax, VA................!(703) 591 5120*24
BBS IBM Hostcomm Fairfax, VA................!(703) 425 9452*24
BBS IBM Hostcomm Springfield, VA............!(703) 425 7229*24
BBS IBM Hostcomm Houston, TX................!(713) 890 0310
BBS IBM Hostcomm Toronto, Ontario, CN.......!(416) 499 7023*24

BBS IBM PC Annandale, VA....................!(703) 560 0979*24
BBS IBM PC Atlanta, GA......................!(404) 294 6879
BBS IBM PC Atlanta, GA......................!(404) 252 9438*24
BBS IBM PC Beltsville, MD...................!(301) 937 4339*24
BBS IBM PC Bethesda, MD.....................!(301) 460 0538*24
BBS IBM PC Billings, MT......................(406) 656 9624

BBS IBM PC California Users Group...........!(805) 987 4127*24
BBS IBM PC Dale City, VA....................!(703) 680 5220*24
BBS IBM PC Denver, CO......................!(303) 773 2699*24
BBS IBM PC Gaithersburg, MD................!(301) 251 6293*24
BBS IBM PC Madison, WI.....................!(608) 262 4939*24
BBS IBM PC New York, NY....................!(201) 678 6670*24
BBS IBM PC Rockville, MD...................!(301) 949 8848*24
BBS IBM PC Vienna, VA......................!(703) 560 7803*24
BBS IBM PCmodem Chicago, IL................!(312) 259 8086*24

BULLET-80 Boston, MA.......................&(617) 266 7789*24
BULLET-80 Chesterland, OH..................(216) 729 2769
BULLET-80 Clarks Summit, PA................(717) 586 2112
BULLET-80 Danbury, CT....................#1(203) 744 4644
BULLET-80 Fayetteville, GA.................(404) 461 9686
BULLET-80 Hawkins, TX......................(214) 769 3036
BULLET-80 Holstein, IA.....................(712) 368 2651
BULLET-80 Houston, TX......................(713) 331 2599
BULLET-80 Ironton, OH......................(614) 532 6920
BULLET-80 Laguna Hills, CA.................(714) 770 5052
BULLET-80 Langhorne, PA....................(215) 364 2180
BULLET-80 Littlefield, TX..................(806) 385 6843
BULLET-80 New York, NY.....................(212) 740 5680*24
BULLET-80 Orange County, Anaheim, CA.........(714) 952 2110
BULLET-80 San Jose, CA.....................(408) 241 0769
BULLET-80 Seymour, CT......................(203) 888 7952
BULLET-80 Springfield, IL..................(217) 529 1113
BULLET-80 Tulsa, OK........................(918) 749 0059*24
BULLET-80 Waterford, MI....................(313) 683 5076*24

CBBS AMRAD, Washington, DC.................(703) 734 1387*24
CBBS Atlanta, GA...........................(404) 394 4220*24
CBBS Baton Rouge, LA.......................(504) 273 3116*24
CBBS Bloomington, IN.......................(812) 334 2522
CBBS Boston, MA............................(617) 646 3610*24
CBBS Cedar Rapids, IA......................(319) 364 0811
CBBS Chicago, IL.........................#1 (312) 545 8086*24
CBBS Corpus Christi, TX....................(512) 855 1512
CBBS CPEUG/ICST Gaithersburg, MD.............(301) 948 5717
CBBS Lambda, Berkeley, CA..................(415) 658 2919
CBBS Lawrence General Hospital, Boston, MA...(617) 683 2119
CBBS LICA LIMBS, Long Island, NY.............(516) 561 6590*24

CBBS London, England..(European standard)..(044) 1 399 2136
CBBS Long Island, NY........................(516) 334 3134*24
CBBS MAUDE Milwaukee, WI....................(414) 241 8364*24
CBBS MicroStar, Worcester, MA...............(617) 752 7284
CBBS NW, Portland, OR.......................(503) 646 5510*24
CBBS PACC, Pittsburgh, PA...................(412) 822 7176*24
CBBS Prince George, B.C., Canada............(604) 562 9515
CBBS Proxima, Berkeley, CA..................(415) 357 1130
CBBS RAMS, Rochester, NY....................(716) 244 9531
CBBS Richfield ? ....(612) 423 5016
CBBS Strictly Software, Honolulu, HI........(808) 944 0562
CBBS TSG, Tucson, AZ........................(602) 746 3956*24

COMNET-80 Akron, OH.........................&(216) 645 0827*24
COMNET-80 Las Vegas, NV.....................&(702) 870 9986
COMNET-80 Mt. Clemens, MI...................&(313) 465 9531
COMNET-80 North Wales, PA...................(215) 855 3809
COMNET-80 Riverside, CA.....................&(714) 359 3189
COMNET-80 Riverside, CA.....................&(714) 877 2253
COMNET-80 Wichita Falls, TX.................(817) 767 5847

CONNECTION-80 Centereach, NY................(516) 588 5836
CONNECTION-80 Denver, CO....................(303) 690 4566*24
CONNECTION-80 Escondido, CA.................(619) 746 6265
CONNECTION-80 Fremont, CA...................(415) 651 4147*24
CONNECTION-80 Gaithersburg, MD..............(301) 840 8588*24
CONNECTION-80 Great Neck, NY................(516) 482 8491*24
CONNECTION-80 Lansing, MI...................(517) 339 3367
CONNECTION-80 Laval BELE, Laval, Quebec, CN..(514) 622 1274*24
CONNECTION-80 Little Rock, AS...............(501) 372 0576
CONNECTION-80 Manhattan, NY.................(212) 991 1664
CONNECTION-80 Orlando, FL...................(305) 644 8327*24
CONNECTION-80 PAUG, Portland, OR............(503) 281 7653
CONNECTION-80 Peterborough, NH..............(603) 924 7920
CONNECTION-80 Tulsa, OK.....................(918) 747 1310*24
CONNECTION-80 W. Mich. Micro Group, MI......(616) 457 1340*24
CONNECTION-80 Winter Garden, FL.............(305) 894 1886*24
CONNECTION-80 Woodhaven, NY.................(212) 441 3755*24
CONNECTION-80 Tampa, FL.....................(813) 977 0989

CONFERENCE-TREE #3, Hayward, CA.............(415) 538 3580
CONFERENCE-TREE #4, Santa Monica, CA........(213) 394 1505

CONFERENCE-TREE Anchorage, AK................(907) 344 5251
CONFERENCE-TREE Computerland, Honolulu, HI...(808) 487 2001*24
CONFERENCE-TREE Flagship, Denville, NJ.......(201) 627 5151*24
CONFERENCE-TREE Kelp Bed, Los Angeles, CA....(213) 372 4800
CONFERENCE-TREE Minneapolis, MN..............(612) 854 9691
CONFERENCE-TREE ?, New Jersey................(201) 627 5151
CONFERENCE-TREE Victoria, TX.................(512) 578 5833

FORUM-80 Augusta, GA........................(803) 279 5392
FORUM-80 Charleston, SC.....................(803) 552 1612*24
FORUM-80 Cleveland, OH......................&(216) 486 4176
FORUM-80 #2, Denver, CO.....................(303) 399 8858*24
FORUM-80 El Paso, TX........................(915) 755 1000*24
FORUM-80 Ft. Lauderdale, FL.................(305) 772 4444*24
FORUM-80 Hull, England..................(011) 44 482 859169
FORUM-80 Kansas City, MO.................#1 &(816) 861 7040*24
FORUM-80 Kansas City, MO....................&(816) 931 9316
FORUM-80 Las Vegas, NV......................(702) 362 3609*24
FORUM-80 Linden, NJ.........................(201) 486 2956*24
FORUM-80 Medford, OR........................(503) 535 6883*24
FORUM-80 Medical, Memphis, TN...............(901) 276 8196*24
FORUM-80 Monmouth, Brielle, NJ..............(201) 528 6623*24
FORUM-80 Montgomery, AL.....................(205) 272 5069
FORUM-80 Nashua, NH.........................(603) 882 5041
FORUM-80 Prince William County, VA...........(703) 670 5881*24
FORUM-80 San Antonio, TX....................!(512) 655 8143
FORUM-80 Seattle, WA........................(206) 723 3282
FORUM-80 Sierra Vista, AZ...................(602) 458 3850*24
FORUM-80 Shreveport, LA.....................(318) 631 7107*24
FORUM-80 Westford, MA.......................(617) 692 3973
FORUM-80 Wichita, KA........................&(316) 682 2113*24
FORUM-80 Wichita Falls, TX..................(817) 855 3916
FORUM-80 Wild goose board, Tampa, FL.........(813) 988 7400

Greene Machine, WPB, FL.....................(305) 965 4388-
Greene Machine Fricaseed Chicken, Arcadia,CA.(213) 445 3591*24
Greene Machine, Riverside, CA...............!(714) 354 8004
Greene Machine Corsair, WPB, FL.............!(305) 968 8653
Greene Machine, Los Alamitos, CA............!(213) 431 1443
Greene Machine, Rome, NY....................!(315) 337 7720
Greene Machine, Irvine, CA..................!(714) 551 4336
Greene Machine, Temple City, CA.............!(213) 287 1363

HBBS Denver, CO..............................(303) 343 8401*24
HBBS El Paso, TX............................(915) 592 1910
HBBS Oklahoma City, OK.....................(405) 848 9329*24

MCMS C.A.M.S. Chicago, IL................#1&(312) 927 1020*24
MCMS J.A.M.S. Lockport, IL..................(815) 838 1020*24
MCMS L.A.M.S. Round Lake, IL................(312) 740 9128
MCMS P.C.M.S. Wheaton, IL.................!&(312) 462 7560*24
MCMS Metro West Database, Chicago, IL.......&(312) 260 0640*24
MCMS NC Software, Minneapolis, MN...........(612) 533 1957*24
MCMS WACO Hot Line, Schaumburg, IL..<pvt>....(312) 351 4374*24

NET-WORKS ABC, Kansas City, MO...............(816) 483 2526
NET-WORKS Apple Grove, Dallas, TX............(214) 644 5197
NET-WORKS Apple Shack, Dallas, TX............(214) 644 4781*24
NET-WORKS Armadillo, Grand Forks, ND.........(701) 746 4959
NET-WORKS Beach BBS, Pensacola, FL...........(904) 932 8271
NET-WORKS Big Apple, Miami, FL...............(305) 948 8000
NET-WORKS C.A.M.S., Decatur, IL..............(217) 429 5541
NET-WORKS Charleston, WV.....................(304) 345 8280
NET-WORKS Chipmunk, Hinsdale, IL.............(312) 323 3741*24
NET-WORKS Coin Games, Los Angeles, CA........(213) 336 5535
NET-WORKS COMM Center NW3NAGAD, Laurel, MD...(301) 953 3341
(301) 792 0305
NET-WORKS Computer City, Providence, RI......(401) 331 8450*24
NET-WORKS Computer Emporium, Des Moines, IA..(515) 279 8863
NET-WORKS Computer Emporium, San Jose, CA....(408) 227 0227
NET-WORKS Computer Market, Honolulu, HI......(808) 521 7312
NET-WORKS Computer Pro, Ft. Worth, TX........(817) 732 1787
NET-WORKS Computer Station, St. Louis, MO....(314) 432 7120
NET-WORKS Computer Store, Honolulu, HI.......(808) 488 7756
NET-WORKS Computer World, Los Angeles, CA....(213) 859 0894*24
NET-WORKS Crescent City, Baton Rouge, LA.....(504) 454 6688
NET-WORKS Dallas, TX.........................(214) 361 1386*24
NET-WORKS Dayton, OH.........................(513) 223 3672
NET-WORKS Eclectic Computer Sys., Dallas, TX.(214) 239 5842
NET-WORKS Granite City, IL...................(618) 877 2904
NET-WORKS Greenfield, IN.....................(317) 326 3833*24
NET-WORKS Hacker-net, Dallas, TX.............(214) 824 7160
NET-WORKS Hawaii.............................(808) 521 7312
NET-WORKS Hawaii Connection, Honolulu, HI....(808) 423 1593*24
NET-WORKS MAGIE, Galesburg, IL...............(309) 342 7178

NET-WORKS Magnetic Fantasies, Los Angeles,CA.(213) 388 5198
NET-WORKS New York, NY......................(212) 410 0949
NET-WORKS North Parks, Chicago, IL...........(312) 745 0924
NET-WORKS Pirate's Harbor, Boston, MA........(617) 720 3600
NET-WROKS Pirate's Lodge ???.................(914) 634 1268
NET-WORKS Pirate's Ship, Chicago, IL.........(312) 935 2933*24
NET-WORKS Pirate's Trek......................(516) 627 9048
NET-WORKS Portsmouth, NH....................(603) 436 3461
NET-WORKS Softworx, West Los Angeles, CA.....(213) 473 2754
NET-WORKS Sparklin' City, Corpus Christi, TX.(512) 882 6569
NET-WORKS Toronto, Ontario, CN...............(416) 445 6696*24
NET-WORKS Warlock's Castle St. Louis, MO.....(618) 345 6638
NET-WORKS Winesap, Dallas, TX................(214) 824 7455
NET-WORKS ???................................(914) 725 4060

ONLINE CDC, San Diego, CA.....................(619) 452 6011
ONLINE Computerland, Montreal, Quebec, CN....(514) 931 0458*24
ONLINE Dickinsons Movie Guide, Mission, KS...(913) 432 5544
ONLINE Indianapolis,IN.<ID#=GUES, pswd=pass>.(317) 787 9881*24
ONLINE Saba, San Diego, CA...................(619) 692 1961*24
ONLINE Santee, CA....<ID#=GUEST, pswd=PASS>..(619) 561 7271*24

PASBBS Torrance, CA.......................#1 (213) 516 7089*24

PBBS Co-operative Comp Svc, Palatine, IL.....(312) 359 9450*24

PET BBS S.E.W.P.U.G., Racine, WI.............(414) 554 9520*24
PET BBS Commodore Comm., Lake St. Louis, MO..(314) 625 4576*24

PMS - **IF**, Anaheim, CA.....................(714) 772 8868*24
PMS - Anchorage, AK..........................(907) 344 8558
PMS - Apple Bits, Kansas City, MO...........!(913) 341 3502*24
PMS - Apple Guild, Weymouth, MA..............(617) 767 1303*24
PMS - Baltimore, MD..........................(301) 764 1995*24
PMS - Campbell, CA...........................(408) 370 0873*24
PMS - Century 23, Las Vegas, NV..............(702) 878 9106*24
PMS - Chicago, IL............................(312) 373 8057*24
PMS - Cincinnati, OH.........................(513) 671 2753
PMS - Computer City, Danvers, MA.............(617) 774 7516
PMS - Computer Merchant, San Diego, CA.......(619) 582 9557
PMS - Computer Solutions, Eugene, OR.........(503) 689 2655*24
PMS - Datel Systems Inc., San Diego, CA.....!(619) 271 8613*24

PMS - Downers Grove/SRT, Downers Grove, IL...(312) 964 6513
PMS - El Cajon, CA............................(619) 579 0553
PMS - Ellicott City, MD.......................(301) 465 3176
PMS - Escondido, CA...........................(619) 746 0667
PMS - Ft. Smith Comp. Club, Ft. Smith, AK....(501) 646 0197
PMS - Gulfcoast, Freeport, TX................(713) 233 7943*24
PMS - Indianapolis, IN.......................(317) 787 5486*24
PMS - Lakeside, CA. (type PMS to activate)...(619) 561 7271*24
PMS - Los Angeles, CA........................(213) 334 7614*24
PMS - Massillon, OH..........................(216) 832 8392*24
PMS - McGraw-Hill Books, New York, NY........(212) 997 2488
PMS - Minneapolis, MN........................(612) 929 6699*24
PMS - I.A.C., Lake Forest, IL................(312) 295 6926*24
PMS - O.A.C., Woodland Hills, CA.............(213) 346 1849*24
PMS - Pikesville, MD.........................(301) 653 3413
PMS - Pleasanton, CA.........................(415) 462 7419*24
PMS - Portland, OR...........................!(503) 245 2536
PMS - Portola Valley, CA.....................(415) 851 3453*24
PMS - RAUG, Akron, OH........................(216) 867 7463*24
PMS - Rutgers Univ. Microlab, Piscataway, NJ.(201) 932 3887
PMS - Santa Cruz, Aptos, CA..................(408) 688 9629*24
PMS - Santee, CA.........................#1 (619) 561 7277*24
PMS - Shrewsbury, NJ.........................(201) 747 6768
PMS - Software Unltd, Kenmore, WA............(206) 486 2368*24
PMS - Twin Cities, Minneapolis, MN..........!(612) 929 8966
PMS - Your Computer Connection, KS Cty, MO..!913) 677 1299

PSBBS Baltimore, MD..........................(301) 994 0399*24
PSBBS Washington, DC.........................(202) 337 4694*24

RATS Systems.............................#1 (201) 887 8874
RATS Homewood, IL............................(312) 957 3924
RATS Wenonah, NJ.............................(609) 468 5293
RATS Wenonah, NJ #2..........................(609) 468 3844

RCP/M A.B. Dick Co., Niles, IL..............&(312) 647 7636*24
RCP/M AIMS Hinsdale, IL......................(312) 789 0499*24
RCP/M Arlington, VA..........................(703) 536 3769
RCP/M CBBS CP/M Net Simi Valley, CA..........(805) 527 9321
RCP/M CBBS Columbus, OH......................(614) 272 2227*24
RCP/M CBBS Dallas, TX........................(214) 931 8274
RCP/M CBBS Frog Hollow, Vancouver, BC, CN....(604) 873 4007*24

RCP/M CBBS Pasadena, CA.......................(213) 799 1632*24
RCP/M CBBS RLP, MacLean, VA..................(703) 524 2549*24
RCP/M CBBS Sacramento, CA...................(916) 483 8718*24
RCP/M Chuck Forsberg, OR.....................(503) 621 3193
RCP/M Collossal Oxgate, San Jose, CA.........(408) 263 2588
RCP/M CUG-NOTE, Denver, CO...................(303) 781 4937*24
RCP/M CUG-NODE, PA State College.............(814) 238 4857*24
RCP/M Detroit, MI............................(313) 584 1044-rb
RCP/M Geneseo, IL............................(309) 944 5455
RCP/M HAPN Hamilton, Ontario, CN.............(416) 335 6620*24
RCP/M IBM PC, Niles, IL......................(312) 259 8086
RCP/M Logan Square, Chicago, IL..............(312) 252 2136
RCP/M MCBBS Keith Petersen, Royal Oak, MI....(313) 759 6569-rb
RCP/M MCBBS Ken Stritzel, Flanders, NJ.......(201) 584 9227*24
RCP/M MCBBS Superbrain, Lexington, MA......$&(617) 862 0781*24
RCP/M MCBBS TCBBS Dearborn, MI...............(313) 846 6127*24
RCP/M Mississauga HUG, Toronto, Ont., CN...$&(416) 826 5394*24
RCP/M NEI, Chicago, IL.......................(312) 949 6189
RCP/M Palatine, IL..........................&(312) 359 8080*24
RCP/M RBBS Allentown, PA.....................(215) 398 3937*24
RCP/M RBBS ANAHUG, Anaheim, CA...............(714) 774 7860*24
RCP/M RBBS Arvada Elect.,Colorado Springs,CO.(303) 634 1158*24
RCP/M RBBS BBS Valley.......................!(213) 360 5053
RCP/M RBBS Boulder, CO.......................(303) 499 9169
RCP/M RBBS Bethesda, MD......................(301) 229 3196
RCP/M RBBS Brewster, NY......................(914) 279 5693
RCP/M RBBS Comp. Tech. Assoc., El Paso, TX...(915) 533 2202*24
RCP/M RBBS Computerized Services, Tampa, FL..(813) 988 7400*24
RCP/M RBBS Computron, Edmonton, Alberta, Can.(403) 482 6854*24
RCP/M RBBS Cranford, NJ......................(201) 272 1874
RCP/M RBBS DataTech 001, San Carlos, CA..#1$&(415) 595 0541*24
RCP/M RBBS DataTech 004, Sunnyvale, CA.......(408) 732 2433
RCP/M RBBS DataTech 006, San Francisco, CA...(415) 563 4953
RCP/M RBBS Edmonton, Alberta, Canada........&(403) 454 6093*24
RCP/M RBBS El Paso, TX.......................(915) 598 1668
RCP/M RBBS Fort Mill, SC.....................(803) 548 0900*24
RCP/M RBBS GFRN Dta Exch. Garden Grove, CA.$&(714) 534 1547*24
RCP/M RBBS GFRN Dta Exch. Palos Verdes, CA.$&(213) 541 2503*24
RCP/M RBBS Grafton, VA.......................(804) 898 7493
RCP/M RBBS Houston, TX.......................(713) 497 5433
RCP/M RBBS Huntsville, AL....................(205) 895 6749-rb
RCP/M RBBS Laurel, MD........................(301) 953 3753*24

RCP/M RBBS Larkspur, CA......................(415) 461 7726*24
RCP/M RBBS Marin County, CA.................(415) 383 0473*24
RCP/M RBBS Mike's, Milwaukee, WI............!(414) 647 0903
RCP/M RBBS MUG, Mission, KS.................&(913) 362 9583*24
RCP/M RBBS Napa Valley, CA...................(707) 253 1523??
RCP/M RBBS Ocean, NJ.........................&(201) 775 8705
RCP/M RBBS Piconet Oxgate, Mountain View, CA.(415) 965 4097*24
RCP/M RBBS San Jose Oxgate, San Jose, CA.....(408) 287 5901*24
RCP/M RBBS Surrey, Vancouver, BC, CN.........(604) 584 2643*24
RCP/M RBBS Pontiac, MI.......................(313) 338 85?5
RCP/M RBBS Paul Bogdanovich, NJ..............(201) 747 7301
RCP/M RBBS Rochester, NY.....................(716) 223 1100*24
RCP/M RBBS Rutgers, New Brunswick, NJ........(201) 932 3879*24
RCP/M RBBS San Diego, CA...................$&(619) 273 4354*24
RCP/M RBBS Sofwaire Store, Los Angeles, CA...(213) 296 5927*24
RCP/M RBBS Software Tools, Austrailia........ (02) 997 1836
RCP/M RBBS Southfield, MI....................(313) 559 5326*24
RCP/M RBBS Westland, MI......................(313) 729 1905-rb
RCP/M RBBS Woodstock, NY.....................(914) 679 8734*24
RCP/M RBBS Yelm, WA..........................(206) 458 3086-rb
RCP/M Silicon Valley, CA.....................(408) 246 5014*24
RCP/M SJBBS Bearsville, NY...................(914) 679 6559-rb
RCP/M SJBBS Johnson City, NY.................(607) 797 6416
RCP/M Terry O'Brien, Vancouver, BC, Canada...(604) 584 2543

Remote Northstar Atlanta, GA..............#1 (404) 926 4318*24
Remote Northstar Denver, CO..................(303) 444 7231
Remote Northstar Largo, FL...................(813) 535 9341*24
Remote Northstar NASA, Greenbelt, MD.........(301) 344 9156
Remote Northstar Santa Barbara, CA...........(805) 682 7876
Remote Northstar Santa Barbara, CA...........(805) 964 4115
Remote Northstar Virginia Beach, VA..........(804) 340 5246

ST80-CC Lance Micklus, Inc. Burlington, VT.#1(802) 862 7023*24
ST80-PBB Monroe Camera Shop, Monroe, NY......(914) 782 7605

TCBBS B.A.M.S. New York, NY..................(212) 362 1040*24
TCBBS Leigh's Computer World, NY.............(212) 879 7698
TCBBS AstroCom, New York, NY..............#1!(212) 799 4649

TRADE-80 Albany, GA..........................(912) 439 7440*24
TRADE-80 Ft. Lauderdale, FL...............#1 (305) 525 1192

TRADE-80 Omaha, NE..........................(402) 292 6184
TRADE-80 Erie, PA..........................(814) 898 2952*24

MORE EXCITING SERVICES

ABBS (?) Queens, NY..........................(212) 896 0519
? (Western Massachusettes)....................(413) 637 3515
Adventure BBS................................(516) 621 9296
All Night BBS................................(213) 564 7636
Alpha, Tampa, FL..<acct#=ABCD00, pwd=TRYIT>..(813) 251 4095*24
Aphrodite-E..................................(201) 790 5910
Apollo's Chariot, Apollo, FL..................(813) 645 3669
Apple-Gram...................................(313) 295 0783*24
Applecrackers, Columbus, OH...................(614) 475 9791*24
ARBB Seattle, WA.............................(206) 546 6239
Armadillo Media Services, Houston, TX........(713) 444 7098
Aviators Bulletin Board, Sacramento, CA......(916) 393 4459
Bathroom Wall BBS, San Antonio, TX...........(512) 655 8143
Baton Rouge Data System, Baton Rouge, LA.....(504) 926 0181
Blue BOSS IBM PC, Berkeley, CA...............(415) 845 9462*24
BBS Annandale, VA............................(703) 978 9754
BBS Apollo, Phoenix, AZ......................!(602) 246 1432*24
BBS B.R., Los Angeles, CA....................(213) 394 5950*24
BBS Computer Applications Co., Poland, OH....(216) 757 3711
BBS Homestead, FL............................(305) 246 1111
BBS Living Videotext, Menlo Park, CA.........(415) 327 8876*24
BBS Metro Detroit, MI........................!(313) 455 4227
BBS Pensacola, FL............................(904) 477 8783
BBS SUE Milwaukee, WI........................(414) 483 4578
BBS The BULL, Toronto, Ontario, CN...........!(416) 423 3265
BBS-80 DALTRUG, Dallas, TX...................(214) 235 8784*24
Big Top Games System, Milwaukee, WI..........(414) 259 9475
Boston Information Exchange, Boston, MA.....&(617) 423 6985*24
Bronx BBS, NY................................(212) 933 9459
Bradley Computer BBS ....(813) 734 7103
BSBB Tampa, FL...............................(813) 885 6187

Capital City BBS, Albany, NY.................(518) 346 3596*24
Carrier 2 Alexandria, VA....................(703) 823 5210
C-HUG Bulletin Board, Fairfax, VA...........(703) 360 3812*24
COMM-80 Queens, NY........................(212) 897 3392*24
Compuque-80, Houston, TX..................(713) 444 7041*24
Compusystems, Columbia, SC................(803) 771 0922
Computer Connection........................(213) 657 1799
Datamate, Canoga Park, CA................#1 (213) 998 7992
Davy Jones Locker..........................(313) 764 1837
Dimension-80 Orange, CA....................(714) 974 9788
Distra-Soft, Montreal, Quebec, CN...........(514) 327 5764*24
Dragon's Game System.........(pass=DRAGON)...(213) 428 5206
Drummer...................................(415) 552 7671
Electric Line Connection, Sherman Oaks, CA...(213) 789 9512
Experimental-80 Kansas City, MO.............(913) 676 3613
Hermes-80 Allentown, PA....................(215) 434 3998
HEX Silver Spring, MD.....................%(301) 593 7033*24
IDBN Info-Net, Costa Mesa, CA...............(714) 545 7359
INFOEX-80 West Palm Beach, FL...............(305) 683 6044*24
INFOEX-80 Akron, OH.......................!(216) 724 2125*24
Irvine Line, Irvine, CA....................(714) 551 4336
JCTS Redmond, WA..........................(206) 883 0403*24
Kinky Kumputer, San Francisco, CA...........(415) 626 5465
Kluge Computer...........................$&(213) 947 8128*24
L.A. Interchange, Los Angeles, CA...........(213) 631 3186*24
Lehigh Press BB, PA......................#1 (215) 435 3388
Lethbridge Gaming system, Lethbridge, AB.....(403) 320 6923
LITHO/NET.................................(800) 831 6964
Long Beach Community Computer...............(213) 591 7239*24
Mail Board-82 Seattle, WA..................(206) 527 0897*24
Micro-80 West Palm Beach, FL................(305) 686 3695
Micro Design, Houston, TX..................(713) 864 4672
Micro Informer.............................(813) 884 1506
Midwest, St. Louis, MO.....................(314) 227 4312
Mini-Bin Seattle, WA.......................(206) 762 5141*24
MOUSE-NET Orlando, FL......................(305) 277 0473*24
MRCBBS....................................(415) 968 1093
MSG-80 Everett, WA.........................(206) 334 7394
NBBS Norfolk, VA...........................(804) 444 3392
NESSY Chicago, IL.......................#1 (312) 773 3308
New England Comp. Soc., Maynard, MA..........(617) 897 0346
New Jersey TELECOM......................#1 (201) 635 0705*24

North Orange County Computer Club............(714) 633 5240
Novation CO., Los Angeles, CA....<pass=CAT>..(213) 881 6880
Nybbles-80 Elmsford, NY.......................(914) 592 5385
Nybbles-80 NY.................................(212) 626 0375
OARCS Portland, Oregon........................(503) 641 2798
OCTUG Orange County, Garden Grove, CA........(714) 530 8226
Ohio Valley BBS...............................(614) 423 4422
Oracle North Hollywood, CA....................(213) 980 5643
Orange County Dta Exchange, Garden Grove, CA.(714) 537 7913
OSUNA Scarsdale, NY...........................(914) 725 4060
Personal Msg. System-80, Deerfield Bch,FL...&(305) 427 6300*24
PET BBS Commodore, Chicago, IL...............(312) 397 0871*24
PET BBS AVC Comline, Indianapolis, IN........(317) 255 5435*24
PET BBS KCPUG, Kansas City, KS...............(816) 356 2382*24
PET BBS SE Wyoming PUG.......................(307) 637 6045*24
PET BBS PSI WordPro, Ontario, CN..........#1 (416) 624 5431*24
PET BBS TPUG, Toronto, Ontario, CN...........(416) 223 2625*24

PHOTO-80, Haledon, NJ.........................(201) 790 6795
PIG-STY Costa Mesa, CA........................(714) 545 4648
PMBBS...(713) 441 4032
Potomac Micro Magic Inc., Falls Church, VA...(703) 379 0303*24
RACS V Fullerton, CA..........................(714) 524 1228
Remote Apple Jackson, MS......................(601) 992 1918*24
SATUG BBS, San Antonio, TX....................(512) 494 0285
Scream Machine................................(312) 680 9613
Seacomm-80 Seattle, WA........................(206) 763 8879*24
SIGNON Reno, NV.................<pswd=FREE>..(702) 826 7234
$(702) 826 7277
SISTER Staten Island, NY......................(212) 442 3874*24
Software Referral Service.....................(603) 625 1919
Sunrise Omega-80, Oakland, CA.................(415) 452 0350
Switchboard, Alexandria, VA...................(703) 765 2161*24
System/80 San Leandro, CA.....................(415) 895 0699
Talk-80 ROBB, Portsmouth, VA..................(804) 484 9636
TBBS Canopus, Milwaukee, WI..................!(414) 281 0545*24
TCUG BBS, Washington, DC......................(703) 836 0384*24
TECOM-80, Tampa, FL...........................(813) 839 6746
Telcom 7 New Fairfield, CT....................(203) 746 5763*24
Telemessage-80, Atlanta, GA...................(404) 962 0616
Treasure Island...............................(313) 547 7903

Twilight Phone..............................(313) 775 1649*24
Vanmil, Milwaukee, WI.......................!(414) 271 7580*24
Visiboard, Wellesley, MA..................!(617) 235 5082
Weekender, Houston, TX......................(713) 492 8700
Westside Download, Detroit, MI...............(313) 533 0254
XBBS Hamilton, OH..........................(513) 863 7681*24
Zachary*Net, Houston, TX....................(713) 933 7353*24

MORE HELPFUL NUMBERS

STATE	NAME & PHONE NUMBER
CA	GFX 408-253-5216 *
CA	IBBS 408-298-6930 *
CA	SOFTWARE CITY 408-866-4224
CO	DENVER 303-758-6233 L
FL	APOGEE 305-238-1231 RL
FL	ST. PETE 813-577-0048 L
IL	INTERFACE 312-296-3883 L
IL	CHICAGO 312-789-3610 *
MA	BILLERICA 617-667-7388 *
MA	STAR BASE 12 617-876-4885 L
MA	NORTH SHORE 617-595-0211 *
MA	YANKEE TRADER 617-937-1976 *
MI	M.A.C.E. WEST 313-274-3940 *
MI	ARCADE 313-978-8087 *
MI	M.A.C.E. 313-544-0885 *#
MI	——— 313-868-2064 R
MI	GRASS 616-241-1971 *
MO	A.U.R.A. 314-894-9243
NJ	J.A.C.G. 201-337-4084
NJ	BAYONNE 201-339-7407 *
NV	L.V. 702-733-9488 L
CA	SYNAPSE 415-527-8276 L
DC	WASHINGTON 202-276-8342 *#
MD	COMPUTER AGE 301-587-2132 L
MD	——— 301-468-6686 L
OK	GREKELCOM 405-722-5056 *
PA	PACE 412-655-2652 *
TX	ACUGD 817-589-1254 *
VA	FUTURE TECH 703-360-5439 *
OR	A.C.E. 503-343-4352 *
GA	ROD ROARK 404-252-9438 *#
GA	GEORGIA 404-434-1168 L
HI	HONOLULU 808-833-2616
WA	WASHINGTON 509-575-7704 L
CO	POOR RICHARD 303-221-1779 L
MD	SEVERNA PARK 301-544-2460 L
NJ	ELEC. CANDY 609-924-5875 L
NJ	BOB ALLEGER 609-267-7825 L#
OH	BCHWOD FLS 216-582-2797 L

ALMOST
FREE
SOFTWARE

ALMOST FREE SOFTWARE

Magazines

Magazines are a valuable resource for the TI home computer owner. The ones we've listed offer program listings to turn your computer into anything from a word processor to a game machine. Informative articles designed to help you get more use from your computer and help you make intelligent software, hardware and book buying decisions are also found in these publications.

Some of the magazines are available on the news stand, some only on a subscription basis. . . but regardless of where you get them you'll find a wealth of 99/4A information and "Almost Free Software".

Write to these publications for more information.

USERS' GROUP PUBLICATIONS

ENTHUSIAST 99
Official Publication of the International 99/4 Users' Group
P.O. Box 67
Bethany, OK 73008

Enthusiast 99 is a complete magazine, available to members anywhere as part of their regular dues. It emphasizes practical applications, listings, and tutorials. Copies can also be ordered from the club at $2.50/each.

TIDINGS
Official Publication of TIHOME
157 Bishopsford Road
Morden, Surrey
England SM46B8

Tidings is a complete magazine that covers TI news of interest to English and European readers. It includes detailed tutorials, listings, and articles on programming techniques.

A group of Australian Users' Group members are preparing *SOFTEX,* a full-scale magazine for publication in Fall 1983. For more information write:

Doug Thomas, National Coordinator
59 Landstrom Quadrant
Kilsyth, Victoria
Australia 3173

The Washington, D.C. Users' Group publishes a 28-32 page newsletter monthly as a service to its membership. For more information, write or call:

Bill Whitmore
Washington, D.C. 99/4 Users
P.O. Box 267
Leesburg, VA 22075

(703) 777-2017

TI PUBLICATIONS

The Texas Instruments Home Computer Newsletter is published monthly for computer users and members of the TI Computer Advantage Clubs.

Questions can be mailed to:

TI Home Computer Newsletter
P.O. Box 10508
MS 5882
Lubbock, TX 79408
ATTN: Editor

GENERAL PUBLICATIONS

99'ER HOME COMPUTER MAGAZINE
Emerald Valley Publishing Co., Inc.
P.O. Box 5537
Eugene, OR 97405

(503) 485-8796 (Editorial Office)

Subscription rates for this comprehensive publication are $25/year in the United States and possessions.

The publication provides both entertainment and business-oriented program listings. Selected programs are also available on cassette tape for $1.00 the first tape and 50 cents each additional order. Foreign orders are shipped airmail—$3.00 for the first tape and 75 cents for each additional tape.

Recognized TI Users' Groups can contact the magazine to purchase these tapes at special bulk terms and rates!

SPECIAL INTEREST PUBLICATIONS

THE COMPUTERIST'S DIRECTORY
15350 River Road
Guerneville, CA 95446

ON-LINE COMPUTER TELEPHONE DIRECTORY
Box 10005
Kansas City, MO 64111

TURTLE NEWS
1208 Hillsdale Drive
Richardson, TX 75081

TI PLUS OTHERS PUBLICATIONS

COMPUTE
PO Box 5406
Greensboro, NC 27403

CREATIVE COMPUTING
Call toll free
800/801-8112

ELECTRONIC GAMES
Box 1128
Dover, NH 07801

INFOWORLD
275 Cochituate Rd.
Box 837
Framingham, MA 01701

KEEPING PACE
466 Rosewood
Pittsburgh, PA 15236

POPULAR COMPUTING
70 Main Street
Peterborough, NH 03458

SOFTLINE
11021 Magnolia Blvd.
North Hollywood, CA 91601

SOFTSIDE
100 Pine Street
Holmes, PA 19043

EDUCATIONAL RESOURCES

FREE (AND ALMOST FREE) SOFTWARE & EDUCATIONAL RESOURCES
For Parents and Educators

Welcome to Free Educational Software

If you are a parent, you want your computer to be more than a game machine—you want it to be a significant part of your child's education. If you are a teacher, you may already have some ideas about the potential of the computer as a learning tool in your classroom. How can parents and educators reach their goals effectively and economically?

One answer is by taking advantage of the public domain educational software and expertise available—for free or at a nominal charge—from educational BBS's and Users' Groups that are springing up all over the world.

Included in these resources are people and organizations that are using the computer to benefit learners of all ages and those who have physical or learning disabilities. With modified equipment and software, computers can enable blind people to "see" and deaf people to "hear". Physically limited individuals can learn to program, do word processing, and "telecommute" to their jobs—even if they can't use the computer keyboard! Students of all ages and levels of ability can learn at their own pace, using computers as an infinitely patient teaching tool.

Computers are equally valuable for exceptionally bright learners. Advanced students can work at an accelerated pace on projects that really challenge them.

In a recent study of learning with computers and TI LOGO, M.I.T. educator Dan Watt observed two students at work on a programming project. One student was brilliant; the other child was considered to be a slow learner. Both students approached their projects in different ways that suited their individual styles and capabilities. Both students succeeded!

This is an exciting time to be a parent, educator, or child. There are lots of people willing to share their enthusiasm, specialized knowledge, and software with you and your family—for free or for a nominal charge!

Computers Help Children Learn

Children learn from every contact with a computer. Even when they're playing an arcade game, they're getting comfortable with the machine, developing game-winning strategies, and improving eye-hand coordination.

What's Educational Software?

Software that has been designed for educational uses—that teaches a subject, improves sequential learning skills, and/or provides a planned learning experience—falls into four categories:

1. Computer-Aided Instruction

Computer-Aided Instruction (CAI) was the first educational application for computers. CAI software teaches through question/answer drills. A public domain game available for the 99/4A, "States and Capitols", is one example of CAI. The commercial "PLATO" educational software series is also CAI.

CAI software can be boring or lively, judgmental or supportive, depending on the person who wrote it.

Good CAI programs take advantage of sound and graphics and provide children with an appropriate reward. Well-written CAI software encourages children and gives them lots of chances to get the right answer. Avoid any program that puts children down or tells them they're "stupid" if they don't get the right answer!

CAI isn't the most creative application for computers in education, but it can be very useful. Your children or students can practice skills and drill themselves on subject matter at their own pace. Computers have lots of patience!

2. Learning Games

Learning games are programs that combine recreational features with sequential learning skills. Their philosophy is to present learning as a game with the kind of sound, graphics, action, challenges, and rewards you would find in a program written for entertainment. Learning games are the hottest new development in commercial educational software. Scott, Foresman and Company's "Mathematic Action Games" are examples of learning games. More learning games will soon be on the market from a variety of educational software developers.

You can also find less sophisticated, but highly enjoyable learning games in public domain software libraries.

3. Simulations

Simulations are programs that "simulate" a real situation, where the child has to make decisions and see the consequences of his or her actions.

"Hammurabi" is a public domain simulation game that puts kids in the role of the ruler of ancient Sumeria. They must make important decisions about economics, crops, and feeding their subjects—or risk an uprising.

Micro-Ed's "Hat in the Ring" is one version of an educational simulation. Students place themselves in the role of presidential candidates. They have to make decisions on media exposure, personal campaigning, domestic issues, and international issues in order to win.

Like learning games, simulations are a new, exciting development in educational software.

4. Programming Languages

A fourth kind of educational software is programming languages designed for children and beginners. TI LOGO is a programming language that is simple and easy to learn, but also has surprisingly sophisticated capabilities for more experienced programmers.

With TI LOGO, kids can write stories, create dialogues, and draw colorful pictures with its "Turtle Graphics" feature, while learning to program. The English-like commands and structured nature of the language create a friendly environment for learning math concepts.

Classroom Management Software

Teachers can also use software that is designed for classroom management to create their own lessons, keep a data base of grades and student information, or do routine record-keeping.

How Can You Get Free Educational Software?

Now that you know what kinds of educational software are available, how can you get it—for free or for a minimal charge?

The rest of this chapter is devoted to organizations and resources that disseminate public domain software to parents and educators. Just as valuable are the bulletin board services, Users' Groups, and publications that allow you to communicate directly with other educators.

These resources will also help you to evaluate software, so you get only the best in public domain or commercial software. An additional valuable feature is the ability to share special needs and experiences in teaching and learning about computers with other educators.

TI Users' Groups

Your first resource for educational software and information is your TI Users' Groups. Almost all of the Users' Groups listed in this book include educational software in their libraries.

The International 99/4 Users-Group

The International 99/4 Users-Group is an international users' group that emphasizes education, as well as games and other kinds of software. Their large library of public domain software includes many excellent educational programs. Charles LaFara, the group's president, estimates that there are more than 400 educational programs available through their software exchange program. No wonder 800 schools belong to the group! (For more information, see the mini-profile on page 58).

The International 99/4 Users-Group also publishes a monthly magazine, *Enthusiast '99,* which is included in the membership dues. The magazine features software reviews, tutorials, articles about TI LOGO, program listings, and other information relevant to educators.

This group is only one example of the TI Users' Groups with public domain educational software. Be sure to read all the Mini-Profiles and to get in touch with your area TI Users' Group. You may be surprised at the educational resources you'll find!

You can get in touch with the International Group's software exchange program by writing or calling:

The International 99/4 Users-Group
P.O. Box 67
Bethany, OK 73008
(405) 948-1023

If you or your school have access to The Source and TEXNET, you can download public domain software from the International 99/4 Users-Group library via modem directly to your cassette or disk. Their electronic bulletin board also features users' groups news, technical information, the ability to "CHAT" with other TI users and educators, and TI LOGO procedures.

YPLA (The Young People's Logo Association)

NOTE: As we were going to press with this book, Jim Muller of the YPLA reported that the group was undergoing some organizational changes. Although some of their services may be curtailed because of financial pressures, the YPLA is committed to keeping their fantastic public domain software library available to TI owners and educators. Read on—whatever new form the YPLA may take, it will still be an excellent resource for TI educators and LOGOphiles.

YPLA is an educational resource organization that supports TI LOGO, as well as versions of the LOGO language, Atari PILOT, and Turtle Graphics on several machines. They also encourage the formation of YPLA Learning Centers all over the world and actively support people and organizations who are using computers to help the handicapped.

YPLA is not completely free—but it's an excellent value. Membership in the organization costs $25 for adults and $9 for students.

Turtle News & Free Software

Once you become a member, you receive the monthly *Turtle News,* which includes programs in TI LOGO. YPLA also offers a program exchange, so you can exchange software that you've developed at home or in school for a free tape or disk of member-contributed programs. Or you can send $10 for a cassette or a disk full of public domain LOGO programs. YPLA now offers a 45-page catalog of public domain software for members—and their library is growing all the time!

YPLA doesn't have a BBS—yet. They're actively pursuing this project so "turtles" all over the world can get on-line with each other.

For more information about YPLA, contact:

James H. Muller
1208 Hillsdale Drive
Richardson, TX 75081
(214) 783-7548

ICCE (International Consortium of Computer Educators)

ICCE is a "grass-roots umbrella organization" dedicated to furthering instructional computing and the effective and proper use of computers in education. Currently, thirty-three educators' groups belong to ICCE with over 15,000 individual members world-wide. Member organizations will soon be linked by a BBS that group officers can access.

ICCE organizes educational conferences and publishes *The Computing Teacher* and many valuable and low-cost booklets for parents and educators.

The Computing Teacher

The Computing Teacher is a valuable journal that is published nine times a year. Each issue is full of application stories by every kind of teacher who uses computers; it also contains programs, reviews, conference announcements, and news. A recent issue featured an in-depth article on how to teach programming, "Some Logo Drawing Ideas", articles by computer-using teachers of learning disabled and handicapped students. . .and more!

ICCE's booklets (in size and contents they are more like small paper-back books) cost from $1.50 - $3.00 for individual copies. They are packed with useful information for parents and educators. To become a member of ICCE, receive *The Computing Teacher,* and receive ordering information for booklets, write:

ICCE Dept. 383
135 Education
University of Oregon
Eugene, OR 97403

Want to form an Educators' group?

ICCE supports the formation of educators' groups and provides assistance and guidelines. If you would like to form an educators' group, or you're involved in a group that would like to join, write or call:

David Moursund, President
ICCE
135 Education
University of Oregon
Eugene, OR 97403
503-686-4414

ICCE does not disseminate public domain software as an organization, but many of their members. (See YPLA, page 162.) There may be an ICCE member group near you!

ICCE Organization Members

Alaska Association for Computers in Education (AACE)
Contact: Kathleen L. Castle, Adult Education
Coordinator, The Northern Institute,
650 W. International Airport Rd., Anchorage, AK 99502
907/563-3174

Alberta Association for Educational Data Systems

Contact: Ann Brebner, President
838 Education Tower, University of Calgary,
2500 University Dr. NW, Calgary, Alberta, Canada T2N 1N4
2061

Association for the Development of Computer-Based Instructional Systems (ADCIS)

Contact: Dr. Gordon Hayes, Executive Director
ADCIS—Miller Hall 409, Western Washington University
Bellingham, WA 98225
206/676-2860

Computer Education Society of Ireland

Contact: Mary Devlin
85 Limetrees Road East, Douglas, Cork, Ireland

Computers, Learners, Users, Educators Association (CLUES)

Contact: Henry J. Petersen, Executive Director
50 Nellis Drive, Wayne, NJ 07470
201/696-3157

Computer-Using Educators (CUE)

Contact: Don McKell
P.O. Box 18547, San Jose, CA 95158
408/288-7642

Computer-Using Educators of British Columbia (CUEBC)

Contact: Barry Underwood
509 Alder St., Campbell River, B.C., Canada V9W 2N9
604/287-8346

Computer-Using Educators of Kentucky (CUE-KY)

Contact: Janet Parker
School of Education, University of Louisville
Louisville, KY 40292
502/588-6431

DIDACOM
Contact: Inno Broekman
Avenbeeck 98, 2182 RZ Hillegom, The Netherlands

Educational Computing Consortium of Ohio
Contact: Ellen Richman, Coordinator
4777 Farnhurst Road, Cleveland, OH 44124
216/291-5225

Educational Computing Organization of Ontario (ECOO)
Contact: Robert E. Drake, President
252 Bloor Street West, Toronto, Ontario, Canada M5S 1V6

Educational Microcomputer Users Group of Central New York (EMUGCNY)
Contact: Jane McCrohan
Roxboro Middle School, Mattydale, NY 13211
315/457-4618 (H)

Educators Interest Group of the San Diego Computer Society
Contact: Melvin L. Zeddies
P.O. Box 81537, San Diego, CA 92138

Florida Association of Science Teachers (FAST)
Contact: Carol Collins, President
15817 Country Lake Drive, Tampa, FL 33624

Idaho Computer Educators' Association (ICEA)
Contact: Jay Larson
Lewis Clark State College, Continuing Education,
8th Avenue and 6th Street, Lewiston, ID 83501

Illinois Association for Educational Data Systems (ILAEDS)
Contact: Lyle B. Smith, President
Computer Science Department, Northern Illinois University,
DeKalb, IL 60115
815/753-0378

Indiana Computer Educators
Contact: David A. Flowers
Ft. Wayne Community Schools, Adm., Cwt.
1230 So. Clinton St., Ft. Wayne, IN 46802
219/425-7228

Manitoba Association for Educational Data Systems (MAN-AEDS)
Contact: E. Boorsma, Secretary-Treasurer
1577 Wall Street, East Winnipeg, Manitoba, Canada R3E 2S5

Michigan Association for Computer Users in Learning (MACUL)
Contact: Lary R. Smith, Communications Sect.
33500 Van Born Road, Wayne, MI 48184
313/326-9300, ext: 562

Minnesota Association for Educational Data Systems
Contact: Sue Talley
1925 W. County Rd BS, St. Paul, MN 55113
612/638-2340

National Institute for Microcomputer Based Learning (NIMBL)
Contact: Stanley Silverman, President
348 Plymouth Ave., Brightwaters, NY 11718

New Hampshire Association for Computer Education Statewide (NHACES)
Contact: Anne Knight, Acting President
University of New Hampshire, Computer Services
Durham, NH 03824
603/862-3527

Northwest Council for Computer Education (Oregon, Washington and Northern Idaho)
Contact: Howard Bailey
Computing Center, Eastern Oregon State College
La Grande, OR 97850
503/963-1582

Oklahoma Educational Computer Users'Program (OECUP)
Contact: Richard V. Andree
Department of Mathematics, 601 Elm St., Room 423
The University of Oklahoma, Norman, OK 73019
405/325-3410

Pennsylvania Learning Resources Association (PLRA)
Contact: George H. Zook, Director, IMS
Lancaster-Lebanon I.U./IMS
P.O. Box 5026, Lancaster, PA 17601
717/569-8561

Saskatchewan Association for Computers in Education
Contact: Duncan Campbell
Mt. Royal Collegiate, 2220 Rusholme Road
Saskatoon, Saskatchewan, Canada S7L 4A4

The Science Teachers' Association of Ontario
Contact: Warren Sirrs
1032 Harness Ave., Ottawa, Ontario, Canada K1V 6P2
613/733-6552

Society of Data Educators (SDE)
Contact: Robert Behling
Bryant College, Smithfield, RI 02917
401/231-1200

Texas Computer Education Association
Contact: Vicki S. Smith
201 Kinkaid School Drive, Houston, TX 77024

The Utah Council for Computers in Education
Contact: Dr. Larry C. Christensen
1295 North 1200 West, Mapleton, UT 84663
801/798-2151

West Australian Computer Educators
Contact: P.C. Farrell, President
12 Lilac Place, Dianella, 6062, Western Australia
276-5891

CUE/SOFTSWAP

Currently, SOFTSWAP does not include public domain software for the TI 99/4A in their software exchange program. As this book is going to press, they are exploring this possibility. SOFTSWAP is still an excellent resource for educational software evaluation and information on how to start a TI Educational Software Exchange program in your County Office or school district.

Computer-Using Educators (CUE) is a California-based group of educators that has over 5,000 members in 49 states, 4 provinces, and 12 nations outside the United States. Because of their active membership and strategic position in "Silicon Valley", California, CUE is in close contact with new developments in the industry. They evaluate new educational software and frequently influence the decisions of manufacturers about educational issues.

CUE also publishes a bi-monthly newsletter and organizes several major conferences per year. CUE's many volunteer workers make it possible for the organization to offer membership and a bi-monthly newsletter for the unbelievable price of $8.00!

Public Domain Software from SOFTSWAP

A joint project of CUE and the San Mateo County Office of Education is the SOFTSWAP project. SOFTSWAP is dedicated to the dissemination of public domain educational software for several of the major personal computers. (See note about TI software, above.)

About one-fourth of the programs are drill and instruction (CAI), but their large software library also includes many creative simulations and learning games. Each "dissemination" disk contains from five to 28 programs for grades K-12.

SOFTSWAP is staffed by four part-time employees, student aides, and lots of volunteers. The project's Chairperson, Ann Lathrop, is a leader in the area of educational software evaluation.

How to get SOFTSWAP Software

There are two ways to get software from this terrific educational resource (if you can't visit their Microcomputer Center in Redwood City, California). One way is to "swap" software by sending your *original* program to SOFTSWAP on disk or cassette tape in exchange for any disk or cassette of your choice. SOFTSWAP welcomes program exchange and is happy to add your original contributions to their ever-expanding library.

Or you can send $1 for their software catalog and order the dissemination disks of your choice for $10 per disk. The cost of the disks pays for copying, mailing, and more free software for educators.

SOFTSWAP is happy to share their software. You are welcome to copy and give away all the software you receive—as long as you give it away for free.

Find out more about SOFTSWAP

To find out more about this wonderful library of free educational software, write:

> Ann Lathrop, Chairperson
> Microcomputer Center, SMERC Library
> San Mateo County Office of Education
> 333 Main Street
> Redwood City, CA 94063

Send $1 for each software catalog. (Listings of new acquisitions are also published in CUE's newsletter and *The Computing Teacher.)*

CUE's Newsletter

CUE's newsletter is also a gold mine of programs, teaching ideas, software and book reviews, news items, product announcements, and discussions of educational issues and policies that are relevant to educators anywhere. To become a member of this dynamic organization and receive their newsletter, write:

Don McKell
Computer-Using Educators
CUE Membership
P.O. Box 18547
San Jose, CA 95158

Send a check to CUE for $8.00 for U.S. membership, $8.00 for Canada, $16.00 for other countries, and $20.00 for institutional subscriptions and memberships.

CUE Welcomes Editorial Contributions

CUE welcomes your editorial contributions. If you would like to contribute announcements, letters, programs, teaching ideas and curricula, reviews of software or hardware, humor, quotable quotes or anything else of interest to computer educators, submit material to:

Dr. Sandy Wagner, Editor
CUE Newsletter
127 O'Connor St.
Menlo Park, CA 94025

An Electronic Bulletin Board for Educators

The Far West Laboratory for Educational Research and Development has teamed up with Computer-Using Educators to create an electronic Bulletin Board specifically for educators. Users can ask questions, exchange ideas, leave messages, and share news about computers in the classroom.

The system is a "Living Tree" BBS. You climb a "tree" of information, branching out to explore areas of special interest to you. To give you an idea of what it's like to talk to a "Living Tree", we called up Far West's BBS for you. Following is a transcript of our conversation with the BBS for educators. Our responses are in boldface type:

AN ACTUAL CONVERSATION WITH THE FAR WEST LABORATORY BBS

—TRANSCRIPT—

INTRODUCING THE LBBS

WITH THE LIVING BBS BEING SUCH A NEW PRODUCT, IT'S LIKELY THAT THIS IS YOUR FIRST VISIT WITH US.

BEFORE GOING FURTHER, YOU SHOULD LEARN HOW TO FREEZE THE ACTION ON THE SCREEN. TO STOP THE ACTION TEMPORARILY, HOLD THE "CONTROL KEY" DOWN AND PRESS "S", FOR STOP. PRESSING "CONTROL-S" AGAIN WILL START THE ACTION.

NOW YOU ARE READY TO BROWSE AROUND THE DATABASE...

WHEN YOU SEE AN ITEM OF INTEREST, TYPE THE NUMBER THAT IS NEXT TO IT, FOLLOWED BY [RETURN]. FOR EXAMPLE, TO SELECT ITEM #3, PRESS "3" THEN [RETURN]. THAT'S HOW YOU GO DEEPER, BUT HOW DO YOU COME BACK OUT?

THE "S" OR SURFACE COMMAND WILL MOVE YOU OUT ONE LEVEL. IF YOU TYPE "7S", YOU WILL MOVE OUT SEVEN LEVELS. THE "S" COMMAND IS VERY IMPORTANT.

THE "M" COMMAND DISPLAYS THE CORRECT MENU. THIS IS USEFUL WHEN THE MENU HAS SCROLLED OFF THE TOP OF YOUR SCREEN.

TO MAKE A NEW MESSAGE, USE THE "N" COMMAND. TRY IT ON THE QUESTIONNAIRE.

READ THE QUESTIONS AND RESPOND USING THE "N" COMMAND.

IF YOU WISH MORE DETAILED INFORMATION, LEAVE YOUR NAME AND ADDRESS IN THE "SYSOP'S" MAILBOX. WE WILL SEND YOU A HELPFUL BROCHURE, EXPLAINING ALL THE COMMANDS.

1:STOP THE ACTION
2:COMMAND MENU
3:THE HELP COMMAND—?
4:TALK TO AN EXPERT
5:HINT: REMEMBER THE "S" COMMAND!

LIVING BBS (Q ? S M N @ X): **@**

[TERMINAL MODE, @@@ TO EXIT]

@@@

[TERMINAL MODE OFF]

LIVING BBS (Q ? S M N @ X): **S**

→SUMMIT OF THIS LBBS

1:INTRODUCING THE LBBS
2:MISCELLANEOUS SECTION
3:QUESTIONS & ANSWERS
4:SPECIAL INTEREST GROUPS
5:BITS & BYTES
6:USER MAILBOXES
7:USER PASSWORDS

LIVING BBS (Q ? S M N @ X): **4**
→SPECIAL INTEREST GROUPS

IF YOU'D LIKE TO START A NEW SPECIAL

INTEREST GROUP ON THIS BULLETIN-BOARD...LEAVE A MESSAGE HERE!

1:OSBORNE 1 USERS AND HOBBY GROUP
2:MORE COMPUTERS IN PUBLIC SCHOOLS!

LIVING BBS (Q ? S M N @ X): **2**

→ MORE COMPUTERS IN PUBLIC SCHOOLS:

FROM: JOHN ALLAIN
MSG #28, 23-FEB-83

I HAVE A FRIEND, HE GOES TO HIGH SCHOOL (SOPHOMORE).
HE IS INTERESTED IN COMPUTERS AND WOULD LIKE VERY MUCH TO HAVE MORE COMPUTERS IN SCHOOL, BUT THEY WON'T LET HIM USE THE COMPUTERS UNTIL YOU GET TO BE A JUNIOR. HIS TALENTS ARE GREAT, BUT THE SCHOOLS WON'T GIVE HIM A CHANCE. I REGRET THIS; I THINK HE SHOULD USE HIS TALENT TO THE TOP OF HIS ABILITY. WHAT DO YOU THINK ABOUT COMPUTERS AND PUBLIC SCHOOLS?

LIVING BBS (Q ? S M N @ X): **S**
→ SPECIAL INTEREST GROUPS

1:OSBORNE 1 USERS AND HOBBY GROUP
2:MORE COMPUTERS IN PUBLIC SCHOOLS!

LIVING BBS (Q ? S M N @ X): **S**

→ SUMMIT OF THIS LBBS

1:INTRODUCING THE LBBS
2:MISCELLANEOUS SECTION
3:QUESTIONS & ANSWERS

4:SPECIAL INTEREST GROUPS
5:BITS & BYTES
6:USER MAILBOXES
7:USER PASSWORDS

LIVING BBS (Q ? S M N @ X): **3**
→ QUESTIONS & ANSWERS

WHEN A PROBLEM OR ISSUE ARISES IN THE CLASSROOM, PRESENT THE TOPIC HERE. POSE YOUR QUESTION AND, PERHAPS, ONE OF OUR OTHER READERS CAN OFFER SOME HELP.

REMEMBER—YOU CAN BE ANONYMOUS. SIMPLY EDIT YOUR MESSAGE, DELETING LINES 0-2 WILL REMOVE YOUR NAME.

WE WANT THIS BULLETIN BOARD TO BE A SOURCE OF HELP TO ALL EDUCATORS. TAKE ADVANTAGE OF THE TECHNOLOGY TO CONVERSE WITH OTHER EDUCATORS. ASK QUESTIONS...OFFER SUGGESTIONS. THIS IS WHAT IT IS ALL ABOUT.

1:WHAT KIND OF GRADEBOOK?
2:EQUIPMENT UNIFORMITY
3:BANK STREET WRITER
4:QUESTIONNAIRE

LIVING BBS (Q ? S M N @ X): **4**
→ QUESTIONNAIRE

WE WOULD LIKE TO KNOW MORE ABOUT THE PEOPLE WHO USE OUR BBS. PLEASE RESPOND TO SOME OF THE QUESTIONS.

1:WHERE ARE YOU CALLING FROM?
2:WHAT IS YOUR TITLE/ROLE?
3:DO YOU USE COMPUTERS IN SCHOOL?

4:IF SO, IN WHAT APPLICATIONS?
5:HOW DID YOU LEARN ABOUT THE LBBS?

LIVING BBS (Q ? S M N @ X): **S**

→ QUESTIONS & ANSWERS

1:WHAT KIND OF GRADEBOOK?
2:EQUIPMENT UNIFORMITY
3:BANK STREET WRITER
4:QUESTIONNAIRE

LIVING BBS (Q ? S M N @ X): **S**

→ SUMMIT OF THIS LBBS

1:INTRODUCING THE LBBS
2:MISCELLANEOUS SECTION
3:QUESTIONS & ANSWERS
4:SPECIAL INTEREST GROUPS
5:BITS & BYTES
6:USER MAILBOXES
7:USER PASSWORDS

LIVING BBS (Q ? S M N @ X): **2**
→ MISCELLANEOUS SECTION

GOT A MESSAGE, BUT YOU'RE NOT SURE WHERE TO PUT IT? THEN PUT IT HERE IN THE "MISCELLANEOUS SECTION"!

1:WHAT IS SOFTSWAP?
2:OTHER BULLETIN BOARDS
3:REMINDERS
4:COMPUTER EVENTS

LIVING BBS (Q ? S M N @ X): **2**
→ OTHER BULLETIN BOARDS

TWO ADDITIONAL BULLETIN BOARD SYSTEMS FOR EDUCATORS:

EDUCATIONAL TECHNOLOGY PEOPLES MESSAGE SYSTEM IN SAN DIEGO (619/265-3428)

THE MEAD SCHOOL FOR HUMAN DEVELOPMENT IN GREENWICH, CT (203/629-4375)

LIVING BBS (Q ? S M N @ X): **S**
→ MISCELLANEOUS SECTION

1:WHAT IS SOFTSWAP?
2:OTHER BULLETIN BOARDS
3:REMINDERS
4:COMPUTER EVENTS

LIVING BBS (Q ? S M N @ X): **4**
→ COMPUTER EVENTS

HERE ARE SOME DATES YOU MAY WANT TO REMEMBER:

MARCH 10-12—THE USE OF MICROCOMPUTERS IN SPECIAL EDUCATION, HARTFORD, CT (703/620-3660)

MARCH 14-15—MACUL '83, DEARBORN, MI (313/326-9300)

MARCH 17-19—FORWARD TO THE 3 C's, TEMPE, AZ (602/965-7363)

MARCH 18-19—COMPUTERS: EXPANDING HORIZONS, AUSTIN, Tx (512/475-2479)

MARCH 18-19—COMPUTERS IN EDUCATION CONFERENCE, SEATTLE, WA (206/334-6965)

MARCH 18-20—WEST COAST COMPUTER FAIRE, SAN FRANCISCO CIVIC AUDITORIUM & BROOKS HALL (415/851-7077)

LIVING BBS (Q ? S M N @ X): **X**

IF YOU ARE COMFORTABLE WITH THE BASIC LBBS COMMANDS, THEN YOU SHOULD TYPE "Y" (FOR "YES"), OTHERWISE, TYPE "N". IF YOU'RE HESITATING. . .GO AHEAD AND GIVE IT A TRY!

ARE YOU AN EXPERT USER (Y/N) ?N

LIVING BBS (Q ? S M N @ X): **Q**

CALL IT A DAY (Y/N) ?Y

CALL AGAIN SOMETIME.
OUR PHONE NUMBER: 415/565-3037

HANGING UP NOW.

Any interested educator or parent who has access to a modem can use the BBS.

Dial:

415-565-3037

If you want to talk to the SYSOP, call:

Kendra Bonnett
415-565-3221

For more information on the BBS, write:

Carolyn Cates/Kendra Bonnett
Far West Laboratory
1855 Folsom Street
San Francisco, CA 94103

More BBS's for Educators

Be sure to read the general chapters on telecommunications: "Read Before Dialing" and "Your Friendly BBS", pp. 109-148 for an overview of electronic communications, a "Modem Buyers' Guide", and other resources.

Bulletin board services and networks for educators are springing up all over the country. The following is a list of additional BBS's that educators with modems can dial up at no charge:

Ed Tech PMS—(619) 265-3428, available evenings and weekends. This BBS is operated by the San Diego State University Department of Educational Technology (and active members of CUE's San Diego chapter).

Kids' PMS—(619) 578-2646, available almost 24 hours daily. This BBS is a message board designed for children. It features jokes, puzzles, and other kid-oriented computer activities. Darlene and Lee Tydlaska are the "Sysops", or system operators.

Notre Dame BBS—(219) 239-5875, operated by Prof. Barry Keating and used principally by students and teachers at Notre Dame. This BBS is also known as "The Leprechaun".

Bullet-80—(203) 629-4375, available 24 hours daily. This BBS is operated by the Mead School for Human Development in Greenwich, Connecticut. The "Sysop" is Bob Jackson.

Other Educational Networks

Educators who telecommunicate may also purchase the following commercial resources:

TEXNET is a special arrangement for TI owners that is operated cooperatively with the SOURCE and the International 99/4 Users-Group.

The TEXNET services most important for educators are:

TI Software Directory—a listing of the latest software available for the TI Home Computer;

TI Graphics Library—a library of graphics programs that you can download to your own computer system;

TI Music and Sound Library—a library of musical programs that provides sounds and scores for your projects;

TI LOGO Exchange—a library of LOGO procedures;

TI Software Exchange—more than 250 programs from the International 99/4 User-Group's public domain library that you can download;

TI Voice Chat—spoken, interactive communications from other on-line users. You can use this optional feature (with Speech Synthesizer) to communicate on-line with other educators.

Members of TEXNET can take advantage of all the services that the Source offers, such as airline schedules, news, sports, current stock quotes, and financial and business information. There are additional services specifically for TI owners. See page 124 for a complete description of all TEXNET services and operating procedures.

For more information on TEXNET, write or call:

TEXNET Information Service
1616 Anderson Road
McLean, VA 22101
(800) 836-3366

EDSIG is the nationwide bulletin board and electronic message center available on Compuserve. EdSig also offers software downloading. The charge is $5.00 per hour, which is billed to your CompuServe account and credit card. Contact a local computer store for information on starting a CompuServe account.

THE KNOWLEDGE INDEX offers access to educational data bases at reduced charges during evenings and weekends. The information includes Psych Abstracts, ERIC, the Microcomputer Index, the International Software Database, and newspaper and magazine databases.

The charge is $24/hour, billed to your credit card. For more information, call or dial:

(800) 227-5510 or (415) 858-3796—California residents.

Also see our section on resources for handicapped computer users on page 194!

THE COMPUTER DISCOVERY CENTER

A different kind of educational resource is now under construction at Six Flags Magic Mountain in Valencia, California. The Computer Discovery Center is a 3,000 sq. ft. facility dedicated to "hands-on" computer learning experiences.

The Center will feature fifty TI 99/4A systems that visitors will operate for educational and entertainment experiences. The Center will also present a short educational film, narrated by Bill Cosby, which explores the history of computers and computer applications.

Software for the Center will be designed for different audiences—children, teenagers, and adult men and women—to ensure that the entire family can participate and benefit from their visit.

Educational Resources From TI

Texas Instruments, Inc., offers support programs for both families and educators—The TI Learning Centers and the TI Computer Advantage Club (TI CAC).

Professional Learning Centers

The *TI Learning Centers* are combined retail/support centers, located in major cities. They are designed to encourage computer literacy and educate TI owners and dealers. According to Mark Sturges, Director of the TI Learning Center in San Francisco, California, the Learning

Center offers a variety of programs for owners of the TI Home Computer and TI Professional Computer. These include:

- hands-on courses on the 99/4A
- classes in cooperation with community organizations, such as the YMCA, Girl Scouts, and community colleges
- courses on the Texas Instruments Professional Computer
- a retail program to sell TI and third-party software
- computer time rental for $5/hour
- software previews for TI owners who want to evaluate a program before purchasing
- a dealer training program for TI Professional Computer retailers
- free noon-time seminars
- training programs for corporate users of the TI Professional Computer

The Learning Centers are staffed by TI employees, including technical and business specialists. The Centers also employ part-time teachers for special programs.

"At the TI Learning Centers, people can see the latest products—everything from calculators to home computers to learning aids," Mark says. "They can also benefit from software demonstrations and our classes and seminars."

TI Learning Centers are now located in Chicago, Illinois; San Francisco, Los Angeles, and Santa Clara, California; New York, New York; and Dallas, Texas.

An affiliated program of the Learning Centers is the TI Computer Advantage Clubs.

Computer Literacy for Schools and Communities

The *TI Computer Advantage Clubs* are centers to promote computer literacy. "Our charter is to spread knowledge about computers, not to sell equipment," states Margie Popkin, San Diego, California, Area Coordinator. "You don't have to be a TI owner in order to benefit from our programs. The knowledge and hands-on experience you gain from our classes are transferable to any computer system."

The Advantage Clubs offer a full range of courses for families, educators, businesses, and schools.

The *Computers for Early Learners* course is for children. Four- and five-year-olds are accompanied by a parent; older children can attend by themselves.

The *Computer Awareness* and *LOGO Discovery* classes are designed for students from seven to fifteen years old.

The *TI BASIC* classes are limited to 10 learners. "We recommend these classes for children who are at least ten years old," says Margie, "because BASIC is a more abstract language than LOGO."

Adult Awareness courses are designed for complete beginners who want computer exposure and elementary BASIC programming skills.

"All the classes are constant hands-on experiences, and every student leaves with handouts and workbooks," Margie states.

Senior citizens who want to attend TI CAC courses receive a discount of 15-50% on fees; families also receive discounts if more than one member attends.

Special Programs for Educators and Organizations

Individual schools or school districts can arrange customized in-service staff training through the TI Computer Advantage program, either on-site or at a central location. "We use lots of educational software in our classes."

There are also systems designed for mobile use that can be placed in an organization for one week to five months. TI Computer Advantage Clubs work in cooperation with other organizations, such as the Boy Scouts, hospitals, and the military, to arrange courses.

"We can arrange discounts on an individual basis for community services," says Margie. "We have worked out special arrangements for some CETA programs in order to bring computer literacy to 1,000 disadvantaged kids in Baltimore, Maryland. Another special program was developed through TI CAC to provide training for paralyzed Vietnam veterans in Florida."

Margie emphasizes that all TI CAC Area Coordinators and the majority of the staff are teachers with credentials both in education and computer instruction.

Long-Term Benefits

Club members receive a quarterly newsletter on new classes and products, with some program listings and educational tips.

"TI CAC courses give people the opportunity to get hands-on experience before choosing a computer, a good overview of applications and practical uses for the computer, an opportunity for schools and organizations to train their staffs, and guided instruction in programming."

TI Computer Advantage Clubs are now located in more than 100 cities nationwide. Courses start at $35 and go up to $75 for advanced material.

For more information on the TI Computer Advantage Clubs, call:

1-800-858-4069 toll-free.

TI LOGO: The Language For Learning

One of the 99/4A's most valuable educational features is TI's version of the LOGO language. As more teachers, parents, and kids become familiar with LOGO, organizations are being formed that provide support and public domain software.

TI LOGO requires initial expenses: a fully expanded system and approximately $130.00 for LOGO II. However, the availability of free software and support groups, and the capabilities of the language can make this a cost-effective investment for parents and educators.

What's So Special About LOGO?

If you haven't already worked with LOGO, you may be wondering what the fuss is all about.

LOGO is a programming language based on an artificial intelligence language called LISP. Seymour Papert, one of LOGO's most influential developers, combined features of LISP with the theories of the Swiss educator and psychologist, Jean Piaget. Papert's main goal, explained in his popular book *Mindstorms* (Basic Books, 1980), is to have children controlling the computers instead of letting computers control children. In the process, children learn problem-solving and come to feel completely comfortable with mathematical concepts.

The result—LOGO—is both a programming language and a learning tool. As a programming language, LOGO is "friendlier" and easier to learn and use than BASIC. BASIC is a more abstract language that children usually can't begin to learn until sixth or seventh grade. Some children (and adults) never really learn how to program with BASIC.

Because of LOGO's friendly English-like commands and "structured" approach, children as young as three and four have been able to program. Some educators believe that LOGO will replace BASIC as a first programming language.

As a learning tool, LOGO helps children to develop problem-solving skills. Kids can enjoy creating graphic designs on their computer screens. At the same time, they are actually learning "structured programming", becoming computer-literate, and seeing geometry in action.

"LOGO is much more than a programming language," says educator Judy Morton of the St. Louis, Missouri, School District. "It's an environment for learning."

Programming Piece by Piece

In LOGO, children construct their programs out of building blocks called "procedures".

A six-year-old child writes a brief series of instructions that draws a "box" on the screen. She then names her procedure "BOX". Every time she wants to use this box shape in a project, she simply writes the command "BOX", and the shape appears on the screen.

She can combine the box with other shapes, make patterns by placing boxes at different angles on the screen, or use "BOX" as a building block for a larger program.

She can easily build a house by combining her procedures, such as "BOX", "WINDOW", and "DOOR".

LOGO encourages kids to break down every problem or project into "modules", "subprocedures", or in plain English, smaller pieces. The child then learns to organize all the pieces in a way that will produce the desired result. They are using structured programming to solve a problem.

The ability to work with procedures that the child creates and names, and the easy English-like commands, are only two of the features that distinguish LOGO as a programming language.

See Geometry in Action

According to M.I.T. educator Dan Watt, part of LOGO's strength comes from the fact that the user controls the computer. "LOGO users can draw on a monitor, create animated cartoons, invent video games and interactive quizzes, or compose poetry and music. LOGO builds a bridge between abstract reasoning and actual experience. . . sidestepping many of the conceptual difficulties people have in learning to program a computer."

One of the features that enables kids to control the computer and see mathematical concepts in action is the "turtle".

The "turtle" is a shape on the screen that you use like a pen. You control the turtle by commanding it to go FORWARD or BACK, LEFT and RIGHT, UP or DOWN. Using these simple commands, you can draw almost any geometric shape.

When a child tells the turtle to go LEFT 90 degrees, he sees the result immediately on his screen. Abstract numbers and angles turn into a concrete object.

Says Watt, "To draw a stick figure of a person. . . a learner encounters many of the key ideas in geometry, algebra, and general problem solving, as well as important concepts of computer programming. Far from being limited to introductory activities, turtle graphics can incorporate the complex mathematical concepts of trigonometry, calculus, and topology."

TI's LOGO II

TI LOGO was developed jointly with Seymour Papert and the MIT LOGO group. It was the first version of LOGO available on microcomputer.

Now, TI is releasing an upgraded version of LOGO—LOGO II.

TI LOGO's most outstanding feature is its ability to "create complex animations using as many as 32 programming sprites." A "sprite" is a shape that can be made to move independently of other pictures on the screen. Using the sprites, kids can send flocks of birds flying across the screen, create starbursts, send rockets into space, and use many other graphics in action. "The availability of 32 sprites in TI LOGO is a feature that is truly unique," says Dr. Judy Morton.

According to Jim Dugan of Texas Instruments, LOGO II contains all the features of the earlier version plus four major enhancements. "LOGO II gives you the ability to use sound and program music; it's RS-232-compatible so you can use it with any printer; it gives you the option of creating large and small sprites; and there is twice as much program-usable space to work with."

Resources and Free Software for TI LOGO

FOLLK (Friends of LOGO, LISP, and Kids) is a San Francisco based non-profit organization that supports all versions of LOGO.

FOLLK's goal is "to spread the word about LOGO and LISP, the languages of learning" to "folk of all ages, interests, and levels of computer expertise." Their projects and services include the FOLLK-Lore Meets, curriculum advising for educators, the FOLLK-Net Bulletin Board System, group and individual workshops in LISP and LOGO, and the unique FOLLK-Flash hotline service.

You don't have to live in California to be "one of the FOLLKs." Out-of-town members can still take advantage of their newsletter and other services.

FREE SOFTWARE

FOLLK has developed a public domain software library that steadily expands. They are also publishing software, such as a LOGO Utilities disk and a LOGO demonstration disk. All the software is available for a small charge or in exchange for your own original contribution.

ANSWERS TO QUESTIONS

FOLLK-Flash is a question-answer service for members. If you have a problem you can't solve, call the FOLLK phone number, leave a message, and a member of the organization will get back to you with an answer within 24-48 hours.

If you or your school has access to a modem, you can dial up the FOLLK-Net, the organization's 24-hour BBS. FOLLK-Net provides a variety of services, including a public message board so you can telecommunicate with other LOGO users.

Regular members pay $25.00/year; students and seniors pay only $15; and institutions pay $100. Subscriptions to the newsletter only are available for $7.50/year.

For more information about FOLLK, write or call:

> FOLLK
> 254 Laguna Honda Blvd.
> San Francisco, CA 94116
> (415) 753-6555

YPLA (Young People's LOGO Association)

See page 162 for information on this invaluable resource for FREE public domain TI LOGO software.

The Center for the Study of Technology in Education

This new organization, based in St. Louis, Missouri, is dedicated to serving the needs of LOGO-using educators.

"LOGO is a learning tool, not an end in itself," states Judy Morton, Director of the Center. "It creates a learning environment where children can really learn to think and to solve problems."

USING LOGO IN THE CLASSROOM

Some of the problems that the Center is endeavoring to solve are the lack of LOGO curriculum activities for teachers. "Everyone talks about the power of LOGO. But how can teachers really use LOGO as a teaching tool in the classroom? We're working on ways that teachers can use LOGO as part of their normal curriculum. We want to support learning with LOGO, not get in the way of the subject matter that the teacher has to cover. Teachers need tools that resemble the SRA reading materials—they are made to be integrated into your normal classroom activities."

The Center emphasizes LOGO tasks that are related to the subject matter that is being taught. One Center project is the development of "task cards". The "task cards" present problems that are related to subject matter and that require simple programming. "The student then breaks the problem down into smaller sections and solves the problem. During the process, the student reports to the teacher so he can discuss problem-solving techniques and receive guidance, if necessary."

For example, children as young as three years old can be introduced both to LOGO and the concepts of left and right. "TI LOGO is especially effective in grades K-5," Dr. Morton says. "One school district I work with has created Turtle Geometry materials for three to five-year-old children who can't even read yet. They made a giant grid out of plastic that the kids can move around on. It works like a combination of a compass and a roulette wheel. The kids learn about left and right, forward and back; learn about numbers by moving a certain number of spaces in each direction; and absorb concepts about angles and geometry. They can then transfer their learning to using Turtle Geometry on the computer.

"The way that TI LOGO uses sprites opens up many possibilities for children—it's an unbelievable learning tool. They can choose and create objects, control their sizes, and make them interact with other objects."

SUPPORT FOR EDUCATORS

Teachers can write directly to the Center to receive materials and task cards and to exchange ideas about ways of using LOGO in the classroom setting.

For more information, write or call:

Dr. Judy Morton
The Center for the Study of Technology in Education
Lindell & Skinker Blvds.
St. Louis, MO 63130
(314) 889-5150

The Micro Computer Research Center

Teachers who live in the Northeastern United States now have an additional resource for LOGO. The Micro Computer Research Center at Columbia University's Teachers College is now offering LOGO courses as part of the Masters program in Computers in Education.

Additional seminars and summer programs, open both to educators and parents, teach LOGO Procedures and introduce gifted young children to computers.

Teachers who live in the New York/New Jersey/Connecticut tri-state area can write to the Center for more information on upcoming classes and seminars:

Ursula Woltz
Assistant Director
The Micro Computer Research Center
Box 18
Teachers College
Columbia University
West 120th St.
New York, NY 10027

For more reading about LOGO, see:

Seymour Papert, *Mindstorms: Children, Computers and Powerful Ideas,* New York: Basic Books, 1980.

Dan Watt, "What Makes LOGO Exciting?", *Popular Computing,* August, 1983.

Also see our section on "Almost Free Software", page 151 for more LOGO resource materials.

FREE RESOURCES FOR HANDICAPPED AND LEARNING DISABLED STUDENTS

Computers offer a wonderful opportunity for people who have physical or learning limitations. As teaching tools, computers are endlessly patient. Modified equipment and software can compensate for physical limitations. Computer software can also be used in novel ways. Word processing software, for example, can enable students who lack fine motor skills to easily express their ideas in print.

Resources For Handicapped Computer Users

99/4 Users of America

This national TI Users' Group is a unique resource for handicapped computer users, especially those who are visually limited. Duane Fischer, Club President, has been totally blind for 18 years. He became interested in the 99/4 in 1980 when he heard that it had voice synthesis capabilities.

Since then, Duane and other club members have developed unique and valuable aids for blind TI computer users. The club offers a "Talking Disk" catalog program, taped manuals and cassette reproduction of important technical material, and special prices for the Text to Speech emulator and TI hardware and software.

Duane has discovered capabilities that even Texas Instruments didn't know about! He can tell you how to use the LIST"SPEECH" command so the computer can read you program listings, line by line. He has also developed an "Error Reader" program that announces error messages to programmers who can't read them on the screen. Duane does sophisticated programming, writes and manages the newsletter, and handles a software exchange and mail order business with a combined voice synthesis/data base program that he created.

99/4 Users of America offers valuable services for any TI user in the United States or Canada, but it's absolutely a *must* for TI Home Computer users with visual handicaps.

For more information about this valuable resource, write or call:

Duane B. Fischer, President
99/4 Users of America
5028 Merit Drive
Flint, MI 48506

(313) 736-3774

Be sure to read the Mini-Profile on the 99/4 Users of America on page 58.

Personal Computer Aids for the Handicapped

The first national competition on Personal Computing to Aid the Handicapped took place recently at Johns Hopkins University. The goal of the competition is to encourage the creative development of hardware and software to aid handicapped people of all ages. For more information about the contest and its participants, write to:

John Hazan
Applied Physics Laboratory
Johns Hopkins Road
Laurel, MD 20810

Texas Instruments and the National Paraplegia Foundation

One of the winners of the Johns Hopkins competition was Jack Kishpaugh, a 99/4A user who is also a paraplegic. Jack teamed together with TI engineer Lee Kitchens to develop modifications for the TI 99/4A that enable paraplegics to communicate with the written word.

With the help of their special keyboard, people who have limited use of their hands and arms can write messages and letters, produce manuscripts, and compose music.

A paraplegic can do all this with only the aid of a headpointer or mouthstick and the modified keyboard.

Individuals with a special need can acquire a modified keyboard by submitting a written request and statement of need to Texas Instruments. TI will try to assist any individual who qualifies.

Write to:

Texas Instruments
Consumer Relations
c/o Tom Shields
P.O. Box 10508
MS 5828
Lubbock, TX 79408

The National Paraplegia Foundation is coordinating other computer-related activities to benefit handicapped people. For more information on their projects, write or call:

Jack Kishpaugh
National Paraplegia Foundation
3400 Hulen
Ft. Worth, TX 76107

(817) 737-6661

ICCE Has Handicapped Resources

ICCE (International Council for Computers in Education) publishes several excellent booklets on computing resources for handicapped and physically limited students.

A Teachers' Guide Book

Learning Disabled Students and Computers: A Teacher's Guide Book is available from the ICCE for $2.50/copy.

A Comprehensive Resource Guide

ICCE also publishes a comprehensive resource guide on *Computer Technology for the Handicapped in Special Education and Rehabilitation* for $7.00/copy. The guide categorizes and summarizes the available literature on computer technology for special education and rehabilitation.

For ordering information, write:

> ICCE
> 135 Education
> University of Oregon
> Eugene, OR 97403

Networking

There are also several networks for learning disabled and handicapped teachers and students.

> SpecialNET (Special Education Community Network)
> National Association of State Directors of Special Education
> 1201 16th St., N.W.
> Washington, DC 20036
> 202-833-4218

> HEX (The Handicapped Educational Exchange)
> Richard Barth
> 11523 Charleton Drive
> Silver Springs, MD 29092
> 301-681-7372

Community Health Information Project

The *Community Health Information Project* is about to go on-line with an electronic BBS for handicapped computer users in cooperation with the Center for Independent Living and organizations for the physically limited and victims of cerebral palsy. For more information, contact:

Joel Yudkin
Community Health Information Project
415-968-8798 (voice)

Deafnet

Deafnet, a government-funded project can provide selected community organizations with public domain software for setting up a BBS for deaf people.

Deafnet is a pilot project to develop and disseminate software for computer communications to deaf people.

Deafnet Brings Computers to the Deaf

"Previously, the whole world of computers—or anything else that uses the ASCII code—was closed to deaf people. One of the goals of our project is to open up that world," states Hal Huntley of SRI International. Many TTD (devices that enable deaf people to use the telephone) were designed to use a BAUDOT code. One of DEAFNET's challenges has been to develop software that translates Baudot into the ASCII code that computers and computer telecommunications use.

The project's goal is to introduce the Deafnet system and train community leaders to use it in 20 major cities in the United States before the project's grant ends in October 1984.

Deafnet can make its public domain network software for the deaf available to selected community groups by special arrangement. For more information, contact:

Hal Huntley
DEAFNET
SRI International
333 Ravenswood Ave.
Menlo Park, CA 94025

(415) 326-2816 (voice) or (415) 326-1802 (TTD)

LOGO and Handicapped Learners

LOGO is a valuable learning tool for special needs and handicapped students. Make sure to read "TI LOGO: the Language for Learning", on page 186, and check our LOGO resources in "Almost Free Software", page 151.

An excellent book on LOGO and special needs students is:

Paul E. Goldenberg, Special Technology for Special Children, Baltimore: University Park Press, 1979.

EDUCATIONAL, ALMOST FREE SOFTWARE

Several publications and organizations offer program listings and software at reasonable costs.

The 99er Home Computer Magazine includes features on LOGO, TI BASIC and educational software, plus program listings. Cassettes of program listings can also be ordered for $1.00 or less from the publication. For information on the *99er Home Computer Magazine,* write:

> *99er Home Computer Magazine*
> P.O. Box 5537
> Eugene, OR 97405

The Enthusiast 99, the official publication of the International 99/4 Users' Group also publishes educational features and program listings. For more information, write or call:

> *Enthusiast 99*
> P.O. Box 67
> Bethany, OK 73008

THE TI COMPUTER ADVANTAGE CLUBS publish curriculum guides, programming activities, and materials for educators and parents. These include:

Computer Awareness for Children—A children's activity book, $5.95.

Programming Discovery in TI BASIC Student Guide—An instructional manual designed to teach programming basics on writing and creating programs, $9.95.

Programming Discovery in TI LOGO Student Guide—TICAC student activities workbook designed to introduce children 8 and older to TI LOGO, $5.95.

LOGO Curriculum Guide—Manual for parents and educators with appropriate activities to encourage problem-solving skills with TI

LOGO. The guide includes lengthy explanations of LOGO commands and comes with one diskette and one cassette, $49.95.

To order TICAC Student and Curriculum Guides, send your check to:

TI Dealer Parts Department
P.O. Box 53
Lubbock, TX 79408

Include $2 for shipping and handling and any applicable state or local tax.

Manuals can be ordered by calling the toll-free Consumer Software Hotline from 8:00 A.M. to 5:15 P.M. (Central Standard Time). Call:

1-800-585-4075

Two noteworthy suppliers of educational software for the 99/4A are Scott, Foresman and Company, and Micro-Ed, Inc. Their offerings range from very reasonable to quite expensive.

Scott, Foresman and Company publishes useful curriculum guides and support materials on TI BASIC and LOGO as well as software. For more information and a complete catalog of TI offerings, write or call:

Scott, Foresman and Company
1900 East Lake Avenue
Glenview, IL 60025

(312) 729-3000

Micro-Ed, Inc., publishes CAI programs, simulations and learning games in TI BASIC and Extended BASIC. Some of their programs start as low as $9.95. For a catalog, comprehensive curriculum guide, and more information, write or call:

Micro-Ed, Inc.
P.O. Box 24156
Minneapolis, MN 55424

(612) 926-2292

PUBLISHED RESOURCES FOR TI LOGO

There are several books available for reasonable prices that offer program listings and activities for TI LOGO. These include:

Donna Beardon, *One, Two, Three, My Computer and Me: A LOGO Funbook for Kids*, Reston, VA: Reston Publishing Company, 1983. Dr. Judy Martin of the Center for the Study of Technology calls this "one of the best resources for LOGO ever written."

Donna Beardon, Kathleen Martin and Jim Muller, *The Turtle's Sourcebook,* Reston, Va: Reston Publishing Company, 1983.

TI UPDATE '84

TI UPDATE '84

TI UPDATE '84
c/o ENRICH/OHAUS
2325 Paragon Drive
San Jose, CA 95131

We're planning to update *Free Software* regularly, but we can't do it without your help!
Please help us keep this valuable resource book current and meaningful for all TI computer users.

USERS' GROUPS

If you've started a new TI Users' Group please let us know the details. We'd also like to know more about activities and developments in your club. If your club publishes a newsletter, please put us on your mailing list!

TELECOMMUNICATIONS

New BBS phone numbers, new products, new telecommunication software—any information that will give future readers the most up-to-date information about this rapidly growing field.

EDUCATION

Please let us know about your new TI educational project(s)—we want to publish this information in the next *Free Software.*

CORRECTIONS

Events change rapidly in the computer field. If you've found any inaccurate information in this printing, we'd like to know. We'll be sure to correct it in our future revised edition.

NEED HELP?

Write to us at "UPDATE '84" and we'll try our best to answer your questions.

YOUR NAME IN PRINT

All contributors to the next issue of *Free Software* will be listed in the acknowledgment section of the book.

BBS DIRECTORY

STATE	BBS NAME	PHONE #	HOURS	PASSWORD /ACCESS CODE